Crystal Clear: A Journey of Self-Discovery

From Public Housing to Ivy League

Crystal Harrell

"How education, both inside and outside of the classroom, gave me clarity and the opportunity to live an abundant life."

SCAN ME

Discover More About Crystal Clear
By Scanning The QR Code Above!

ISBN: 978-1-7367786-0-9 (Paperback)

ISBN: 978-1-7367786-2-3 (eBook)

Library of Congress Control Number: 2021915599

Crystal Clear: Innovation Through Education

New Haven, CT 06511

https://crystalclearinnovation.com

For speaking engagements or signed books, contact the author at

contactme@crystalclearinnovation.com

Cover designer: Alejandro Ariel Martin, https://www.bloom-designagency.com/

Editor: Margaret A. Harrell, https://margaretharrell.com

Dedication

To dreamers everywhere. It is possible. Use your passion, creativity, and whatever knowledge you possess to take action. Taking action is how dreams are made and progress is realized.

One must know oneself. If this does not serve to discover truth, it at least serves as a rule of life and there is nothing better.

—*Blaise Pascal*

Contents

Introduction 1

Chapter 1: Know Your Roots.................................... 7

Chapter 2: My Family Situation and Childhood Trauma ... 27

Chapter 3: Against All Odds 39

Chapter 4: When I Grow Up 51

Chapter 5: Make the Sacrifice................................ 67

Chapter 6: The Value of a Dream 83

Chapter 7: The Promised Land................................ 89

Chapter 8: Push Past the Barriers 99

Epilogue 107

Acknowledgments 111

About the Author... 113

Introduction

Belief in God is my greatest asset, but also, is the belief in myself.

—Crystal Harrell

Your beginnings will seem humble, so prosperous will your future be.

—Job 8:7

*F*or a long time, I was ashamed of my story. I never wanted to talk about it. About those humble beginnings, those painful humble beginnings. To be honest, this book has been a work in progress for several years. Not because I did not have the words to say but because I lacked the confidence to say them. I thought: *If people really knew where I came from or what issues I battled practically since birth, they would look at me so differently. They would not like me, or they would think that I wasn't good enough.*

I was so ashamed, projecting my insecurities onto others, putting the beliefs in my head about what they would think of me into theirs. This caused me to be silent and not share my story with those that could have benefited from it. When I was a senior in college, my mother said to me, "Baby, you struggle with anxiety because you have so much to say and you never do."

That was the changing point for me. I decided that in order to help others and myself, I would be *grateful for my beginnings* because they made me who I am today. I decided to tell my story. In this book, I will walk you through my journey of self-discovery. I will show you how self-awareness led to my healing and ultimately to a life so fabulous I could not have imagined it—a life filled with numerous blessings and financial stability. I cannot show you THE way, but I can show you *a* way. I can show *you how I was able to rise against all odds and live an abundant life.* One that is constantly expanding to reflect the internal abundance I feel daily.

When looking back, I think about those very early days growing up in a public-housing apartment in rural Alabama with nine other siblings. I never imagined life any other way. It was not until after a tragic event happened in my life that I began to see that things could be different. After tragedy came clarity, and I began to become intentional about my growth and personal development. I started seeing possibilities for my life expand as I gathered more and more knowledge about scores of individuals who went from humble beginnings (like I had) to prosperous futures. I see now that my beginnings developed my character in ways it would not have manifested otherwise. A young girl from a small town, once she got big dreams, became a woman with vision!

I love the story my mother tells me about her friend's dream before I was born. She was working at a Golden Corral in Liberty City, one of the most dangerous neighborhoods in Miami, Florida. That day, my mother went to work, just as she had on any other day. However, only a few minutes after my mother clocked in, her close friend, Ms. Stori, stopped her to talk. Ms. Stori was a tall, thin woman who wore her jet-black hair cut short. She had beautiful brown eyes.

Ms. Stori, in some excitement, then told my mother, "I had a dream last night that you were standing next to this beautiful river. The water was so crystal clear that you could see right through it. While you were standing next to this river, there was a little girl next to you who was holding your hand. She had light brown skin and was so pretty. You should have seen this river, Elaine!" she exclaimed. "It was so crystal clear!" At that moment, almost no one knew my mom was pregnant. Only she and my father.

They were waiting to share the news until my mom was further along. After Ms. Stori finished narrating the dream, they both paused briefly. I think at this moment my mother paused in order to contemplate it, and Ms. Stori was most likely waiting for my mother to confirm or deny what she felt to be true. Then my mother admitted with a soft grin, "I'm pregnant." Ms. Stori could hardly contain her joy as she spoke. "I knew it! I knew!" My mom waited for the excitement to die down and added, "I go in for an ultrasound in a few weeks, and if it is a girl, then I will name her Crystal."

I was that little girl with my hand in my mother's as we stood next to that beautiful crystal-clear river that flowed seamlessly. My mom tells me that my life is meant to flow just like that river, and though dams form and obstruct the flow, they will eventually diminish, and the river will flow again. The title of this book, *Crystal Clear*, reflects my journey to understanding the fulfillment of my life and my purpose on earth. I believe I am meant to provide clarity and help others discover their flow, which at the same time, will help maintain mine. God has blessed me with the realization and wisdom of my Truth at a young age. I know that I still have a lot to learn on this journey, but I am setting out with a strong foundation in faith that eventually all things will be revealed. If you want to find out what your purpose is, then you will have to be honest with yourself and study your passions.

The late Bahamian evangelist and ordained minister, Dr. Myles Munroe, pointed out in a 2004 seminar that your existence is evidence this generation needs something your life contains. Just like God placed the seed inside the tree, He also placed the fullest expression of who you are meant to be somewhere He knew you would not miss it. He placed it inside you. We have everything we need to live a full and abundant life right here, right now. The technology to build airplanes, computers, skyrises, and every great wonder of this world has always been available to us. It only took wisdom, invention, and understanding to get to it.

I found my Truth in spirituality and universal law, and after reading books like *Think & Grow Rich* by Napoleon Hill and *The Power of Positive Thinking* by Norman Vincent Peale, I realized just how powerful universal law can be. I started to invest in personal-development books and YouTube videos that offered spiritual guidance like those of the late Dr. Wayne Dyer. I followed successful people and researched their lives, but not just any successful person. I wanted to learn more about your typical "rags to riches" stories. I wanted to find out how those individuals managed to beat the odds and conquer everything stacked against them. During this investigation, I noticed patterns.

I had found the secret to success and realized it was no secret at all. It was a formula, and the successful people who went from struggling in poverty to being surrounded by luxury and opportunity had only tapped into the *mindset* that revealed this formula to them. The secret to success is actually a *system of success*. I want you to remember that word—system—because throughout this book I will reveal parts of that system that helped me on my journey.

Note that information and education alone do not cause transformation. It is the application of that knowledge (a.k.a. wisdom) that causes the transformation. Education has been described as the ability to meet life's situations. Its main goal is not knowledge but ACTION. So, school—the traditional educational system—may not be for everyone, but education is.

How you get that education is up to you and what fits your needs. We have seen time and again successful people drop out of school and end up very wealthy. Take, for instance, Bill Gates. However, Bill and Melinda Gates formed a scholarship program that, by the time it ended in 2016, had sent over twenty thousand minority students to college, fully funded, in any program they were accepted into in the United States. If he did not think education played an important role, then I am sure that he could have found something else to invest that money into.

Once in an interview, Bill Gates said he wanted to see if minority students who showed academic promise in high school could do well in higher education if finances were not an issue. After years of analysis, the Gates Foundation found that not only do these students do well, but their performance level typically exceeds that of other students. I am one of those twenty thousand students that Bill and Melinda Gates sent to school on a ten-year full-ride scholarship. I one day hope to meet the Gateses and thank them because now I have the means to accomplish my dreams and give back to my community.

During my first semester in graduate school at Auburn University, a professor looked at me and said, "You know, students of color usually fail in school due to lack of mentorship and lack of investment." He said this to me because I made a mistake in my outreach email to him; it was not professional enough, he told me.

I was extremely offended, but I realized something then. I had the ability to invest in students of color, especially those who are first-generation college students like me. I can share with them everything I learned on my journey so they will not have to make similar mistakes. The truth is, we are doing our best to navigate a system designed to keep people like us out. My mom once told me, "God is using you to show others that there is always a way out." Her words have since been my guiding light whenever I am in a dark tunnel of despair. My mission is simple. To use my story and the tools of success I acquired to create change and help make that path to change CRYSTAL CLEAR.

I became a certified Academic Success Coach in 2019, and I encourage my students to go after what they are passionate about, even if they think it will not make them any money, even if they have hit wall after wall. I do this because your passion is your calling, and when you are walking in your calling, doors will open. When a Yale professor, Dr. Yusuf Ransome, said to me, "I could use your passion and drive in my lab," after the first conversation I had with him about my research interests, I knew then that passion was undeniable. People do not ignore passion because it speaks to the spirit. Passion keeps you up at night when you cannot stop thinking about a new idea; it wakes you up early—you sleep, eat and breathe your passion. People are attracted to it because passion gets results. It is that simple.

At the end of each chapter, I lay out action steps and ideas worth noting. Write them down and plan a day and time when you will apply them. Only take the ones that speak to your Truth, those that resonate with your Divine Purpose. You were made to fulfill a great purpose in this life. You are the only one who knows what that purpose is and whether you are aligned with that purpose at this very moment. There is no substitute for self-awareness. I will remind you of this several times because repetition is the mother of all learning.

Chapter 1

Know Your Roots

> Armed with the knowledge of our past, we can with
> confidence charter a course for our future. Culture is
> an indispensable weapon in the freedom struggle. We
> must take hold of it and forge the future with the past.
>
> —*Malcolm X*

In order to know where you are going, you must first understand where you have been. I decided that if I were to tell my story, then I have to start at the beginning. As far back as I can go.

Do you ever wonder about the people who passed down their genes to you? Where did you get your nose or that quirky laugh? There is nothing lost in the genetic code. Genes can, however, become mutated or evolve, and certain genetic expressions happen in the context of triggers present within a given environment, but nothing is lost. By using a technique called "Recombinant DNA," which identifies, maps, and sequences genes to determine their function, scientists have discovered that genes can and do change. They also adapt and reform in accordance with opportunities to do so. What our grandparents experienced (on all levels) is somehow imprinted and recorded in their grandchildren's genes and so forth. Who you are is in part a combination of your ancestors and what made them.

A few years ago, my cousin Devin gifted me an Ancestry DNA kit because he knew I wanted to learn more about where I came from. Knowing that getting the DNA test would allow me to confirm what I was finding in the paper trail my ancestors left behind, I agreed. When my results came in a few weeks later, I saw that what I was finding in the documents was correct. My DNA was traced along the east coast of the United States, starting in North Carolina and ending in Florida. However, I had not been able to trace my ancestry outside of America, so I was really shocked to see the international sites.

I knew that most of my ancestry would be traced to West Africa because most enslaved persons from the transatlantic slave trade were shipped from there. Most of my DNA was from Nigeria (42 percent) and the second-largest place was Cameroon, Congo, and Western Bantu Peoples (23 percent). I also knew that some of my ancestors were European. The third-largest chunk is from Europe, in particular, England, Northwestern Europe, Spain, France, Norway, and Scotland (17 percent). I am an adventurer at heart, so I always thought it would be cool to one day visit every region my DNA was traced to.

There is no better feeling than to learn about who you are. This realization and the process of getting to know yourself are liberating! We all have aspects of ourselves that we are not proud of, or that we wish we could change. But wouldn't it be something to know that a personality trait you have was the same one your third-generation grandmother had? If you want to know who you are, then start with your ancestors. Even the Bible speaks about the importance of Jesus Christ's lineage. If it was not of importance, then it would not have been mentioned. I encourage you to learn about your ancestors, celebrate your family traditions, embrace your culture, and develop a greater sense of self in the process. You will not regret it. You must look backward in order to look forward to the future and the possibilities that await you.

When I was eleven, I had a dream that I met this little boy. He was maybe six or seven, but I remember his clothes being a little too small and his shirt barely covering the entirety of his stomach because of his large-for-his-age size. He was slightly overweight but energetic. I did not know the little boy's name. He never told me, but he was talking a lot, trying to show me things. Then the little boy led me to a dark cave. The sound of water dripping in the distance echoed throughout. Inside the cave was an older woman. She seemed malicious. Almost instantly I knew she was a witch. However, as we watched her stir her brew, she could not see us. I was not afraid but realized that if she saw us, it would mean trouble. After what felt like five minutes in which we watched the malicious woman work, the little boy grabbed my hand and looked up at me with enthusiasm in his eyes. "I have to show you something," he said.

I smiled softly and agreed because I was still anxious about being seen by the witch if we stayed any longer. However, where he took me this time was to the past. He showed me what I understood to be past generations. I could see all of my ancestors so clearly.

The last generation he showed me was of a native man—very thin, with almost yellow skin. His hair, cut in a bowl shape, was the darkest shade of black I had ever seen, resembling the black of a raven's wings that from certain angles almost looks purple. Draped over the thin man's shoulders was a sack; the mouth of the sack was open behind him as he picked fruit from a dark green bush. Just as the man was turning around, my dream ended. Puzzling over who the little boy was, I lay awake, unable to sleep again.

I immediately, the next day, told my mom the dream, and as I described the little boy, she gasped. "That was your father," she told me. "When he was a little boy, he was *so* big, that's how he got the name Hubert. The way you described this little boy is exactly how his family described your dad as a child." My dad had passed away a few months prior, and I have been unable to forget that dream.

Fast forward ten years. Immersed in genealogical research as a college junior, I had no intention of becoming the family historian, which I was so promptly labeled. I just loved asking questions about my past and finding those answers through documents and family stories. I became a member of the Afro-American Historical and Genealogical Society while doing this research, the youngest member there by at least twenty to thirty years. I always wondered why my generation never seemed interested in learning about their ancestry.

As you learn more about your roots, you will begin to develop a sense of nostalgia. A sad feeling is commonly present but is quickly replaced by hope. No matter the bloodline, you will find a history of resiliency. *You are your ancestors' wildest dreams.* I encourage you to learn more about your ancestry.

Start with your parents and go from there. Ancestry.com is a great place to start as well, but if you do not have the means, then it is possible to ask questions from relatives. I will guarantee that there is an aunt or other family member who knows more about the family history than you could imagine. Do not wait. Start today because the longer you wait, the more difficult it may become to get information. The first step to knowing anything is by asking the right questions. Write down what you find and photograph the documents. Start writing the story of your past if it has not been recorded already because that written story can be passed down through generations.

Finding My Way

I moved to New Haven in June 2020. And once there, I could not shake the feeling of nostalgia. I kept telling people it felt like I had been there before. Even my very first visit to New Haven, when I was invited to interview for Yale's PhD program, felt strangely familiar. I had never stepped foot in the state of Connecticut previously, but I felt like I was returning home.

On December 21, 2020, I was restless. I had been completely exhausted that entire day but found myself unable to sleep that night despite my best efforts.

As an undergraduate I was trained by my statistics professor and now mentor, Dr. Robert Bubb, on how to conduct genealogical research. Dr. Bubb worked as a statistics professor, having completed his doctorate in Industrial and Organizational Psychology, but he had a passion for genealogical research. He headed projects in the department at Auburn University that reconstructed the African American family unit through genealogical research. Currently, he works to preserve the African American cemeteries in an area where they had previously been abandoned.

Dr. Bubb would take me to various courthouses, giving me advice on how to piece together family trees. "Sometimes past lives will speak to you," he said as we shuffled through old deeds, "Everyone wants their story told." I will never forget the way it felt, being inside of the Lagrange County Courthouse basement, searching for deeds and other documents that could help reconstruct the story of a family I was assigned to research that semester, the Escoe family. When you would walk into these places, you are immediately hit with the smell of old paper and glue that many decades prior lost its functionality. However, there was always a familiar feeling inside those walls, being surrounded by a plethora of stories waiting to be told.

Ancestors, I feel, have a way of speaking to you beyond the grave if you are willing to listen. They want their stories told because their life has significance beyond their death. Think about how complex and multifaceted your life has been up to this point. Do you think someone could write out even the most interesting details in a single book? It would be impossible to record your day-to-day life on mere pages of a book. However, having just your name remembered after your death and passed on through generations would be an honor. No one wants to be forgotten, even after life has ended. There is a reason why we are so protective of our namesakes. I thought, "The least I can do is find out my ancestors' names. Anything I find out about the details of their life would be a blessing and more than what I expected."

When I started graduate school, I retired the title of "family historian." The thing about genealogical research is that it is very time-consuming and difficult to pull away from once you find a clue or piece to the puzzle. It can also be frustrating when you hit several walls. However, on December 21, 2020, my ancestors had once again urged me to return to genealogical research. While tossing and turning that night, I felt almost obligated to somehow distract my mind so that I would not cry out of frustration. I instinctively knew that it was time to start learning more about where I came from.

In the past, I would spend days researching a single ancestor, but that night the information was flowing. I started with my paternal ancestry. I always felt as if it was important to learn more about my dad's side. What were their names? Where did they live? Did any of them have my dad's mannerisms? Could they tell me more about my dad's personality when he was younger? Several hours had passed and the sun was coming up before I realized that I had discovered the names of my third great-grandparents (the "third" means there are three "greats" in front of "great-grandparents"). This is the language used on ancestry-research websites and means my great-great-great-great grandparents. "How was this possible?" I thought. "I could never find this information before. What made that night so special?" The only explanation I can think of is that it was meant to be. It was time to learn more about who I was. 2020 had been a year of clarity, so this was the final door I had to unlock before the end of the year.

The Harrell Lineage

Wiley and Sina Harrell were two enslaved persons living in Hawkinsville, Georgia, in the early 1800s. During the 1800s, cotton reigned as the lifeblood of Georgia's economy. Wiley was born in 1801 and Sina in 1807 on the Harrell plantation. In my family's stories and in the slave narratives by neighbors, the Harrell slave owners were described as relatively "sensible" and "less adversarial," compared to others, but we in my present-time family always agreed that the practice of slavery was awful. Therefore, being treated as a human by slave owners was no honorable act. Together, between 1836 and 1847, Wiley and Sina had one son and two daughters. Prior to 1865, it was unlikely that enslaved persons would show up on any census records with names and residences. The 1870 federal census was the first to list the ages, names, and occupations of slaves. However, Wiley, Sina, and their three children were all recorded in an 1850 United States Federal Census for Pulaski County, Georgia, with several other families—for example, the Frasers, Downmans, Francises, McFails—plus other Harrell families in the area.

The Wiley residence was listed as Division 69, Dwelling no. 168. Wiley worked as a farmer, but Sina did not have an occupation listed. Usually, the woman is recorded as a "domestic servant." Forty-nine-year-old Wiley and forty-three-year-old Sina and their three children— Eliza (fourteen), Gilphy (twelve), and Joseph (six)—were all residents of Dwelling 168, with someone named Martha Harrell (thirty-four) also living with them. I have yet to find out who Martha was, but I am still searching.

Their youngest child, Joseph Levi, my great-great grandfather, who took the first and last name of one of his slave owners, was born in March 1847. He later married Laura Lampkin Harrell, born in

September 1860, and they had nine children together. Laura is the mulatto daughter of my enslaved ancestor Rosa Harrell and one of the Harrell slave owners. Laura had a lot of terrible experiences growing up but never talked about her time in slavery much. There is a black-and-white photograph of Joseph and Laura taken around 1900. Joseph's beard is all white, and his soft hair is cut low.

Pictured: Laura Lampkin, Joseph Levi, and Annie (Touie) Harrell (circa 1900)
Former enslaved persons in Pulaski County, Georgia

Strangely enough, Joseph has the same face and hands as my father. When I first witnessed the photograph of Joseph, I instantly felt connected to him. My family always joked about how strong the Harrell genes were and seeing this photograph was proof. Joseph is wearing a clean white shirt underneath a tattered leather jacket, but the tattered jacket simultaneously somehow looks brand new. His left hand is resting in his lap, slightly tucked behind one of his daughters, Annie—also called Touie—who was around three or four. Annie is wearing a beautiful white dress, with her little arms folded across her lap. She is staring directly at the camera and has her soft, curly hair parted down the middle and cut to her shoulders. Laura is also staring directly at the camera and has her hair parted down the middle just like Annie's, but it is pulled back into a low ponytail. Her eyes seem tired but content. Her beautiful white shirt and nicely pressed skirt draw your eyes to them.

The most significant aspect of this photograph is the attire of Joseph, Laura, and Annie. Joseph and Laura were born into enslavement but managed to live successful lives during one of the most difficult times in American history, the Reconstruction Era. Joseph was a farmer and businessman who hired labor to help repair the farmland and had been a Civil War prisoner of war from January 22 to February 18, 1865, when Fort Fisher was captured by the Union Army. He learned how to read and write, sent their children to school after the end of slavery, and successfully managed his business.

Their attire in the 1900 photograph is an indication of his business success in Pulaski County, Georgia. Harrell descendants of slaves in my family still own land in Georgia, and there is a Harrell cemetery in Pulaski County as well. The slave owner of Joseph gifted him a leather wallet as a freedom gift when slavery ended. I and my family often wonder what type of relationship existed between Joseph and his slave owner that made him give him a wallet and pass down so much land. I imagine that my great-great-grandfather was a talented businessman because he never lost the land or wallet that was given to him. It has all been passed down through generations.

It is difficult to imagine how life may have looked during the time my ancestors were enslaved in Pulaski County, Georgia, but I believe this story from the Federal Writers' Project that collected slave narratives during the Reconstruction Era could help illustrate. *Born in Slavery: Slave Narratives from the Federal Writers' Project, 1936–1938* contains more than 2,300 first-person accounts of slavery and five hundred black-and-white photographs of formerly enslaved persons. Bob Mobley was a ninety-year-old former enslaved person from Pulaski County in the same location as my third and second great-grandparents were reported to have lived. Bob recounts:

> Grown negro men, in those days, wore their hair long and, as a punishment to them for misconduct (etc.), the master cut their hair off . . . If a slave became sick, a doctor was promptly called to attend him. My mother was also a kind of doctor and often rode all over the plantation to dose ailing negroes with herb teas and medicines which she was adept in compounding.

Bob later moved to Hawkinsville, Georgia, where he started work as a carpenter until he fell off a roof and was unable to work. I wonder if he and my ancestors knew each other since Hawkinsville is a small rural town. His story gave me more insight into what daily life may have looked like for my ancestors during their time in bondage.

One of the nine children Joseph and Laura had together was James "Jim" Harrell, my great-grandfather, born on December 12, 1897. Jim was a mulatto man (as listed in the census records according to his skin complexion and lineage) who lived in Georgia and joined Harmony Baptist Church at a young age. There he served as a deacon and treasurer until his death on October 21, 1981, a few months shy of his eighty-fourth birthday. Jim was no stranger to intense labor, having worked as a farmer from the young age of thirteen. A World War I Draft Registration Card on June 5, 1918, described twenty-one-year-old Jim as tall and slender with black eyes and black hair. At the time of the draft, Jim was employed by William Byrd Daniel, a dealer in livestock in Pulaski County. Jim also married Annie Lou Harrell at the age of seventeen, and in 1930 the two lived on a farm where he rented his home in Pulaski County with two daughters, Annie L. (twelve) and Luna B. (four), son Jack (seven), and two brothers-in-law, Monroe Offlin (nine) and Cartell T. Edwards (nineteen).

Now for my grandparents. On October 26, 1923, Jim had Henry Louis Harrell with Tommie Lee Jackson in Hawkinsville, Georgia. Henry, my grandfather, married Bertha James-Harrell, my grandmother, and the two raised several children together. I have seen pictures of me standing next to my grandfather, but I have no memory of him or my grandmother Bertha. My older siblings speak of them fondly. Bertha was born on November 4, 1922, and was the daughter of Burrell and Juliann James from Eastman, Georgia. Bertha's father, Burrell, was the son of Mitchell James and Harriette Byrumm. Bertha's mother, Julianne, was the daughter of Woiciecb Kolacki and Acki Koi. Julianne, my father's maternal grandmother, was half Polish and half American Indian and worked as a midwife until her later years.

Henry had a sixth-grade education and worked as a sharecropper in Georgia, but one day he got into a confrontation with one of the white landowners. In the heat of the moment, Henry struck the landowner. Out of fear for his life, he fled to Miami, Florida. Henry and Bertha raised the remaining children together in Florida and lived there until their death. My grandfather, Henry, died on October 29, 2004, at North Shore Hospital in Miami, and my grandmother, Bertha, died on September 7, 1997. She is buried at Southern Memorial Park.

One of the children Bertha and Henry raised together was my father Hubert "Stein" Harrell, born on June 12, 1949. Hubert got his name because he was an oversized baby when born. Growing up, Hubert maintained an interest in books and studying, and his friends and family would remark on his natural intellect. As a teenager, he got the nickname "Stein" (short for "Einstein"), a name he went by his whole life. I did not know Stein was my father's nickname until his funeral when I saw "Hubert Harrell" in the obituary.

My father was a Vietnam veteran and served in the United States Army from September 23, 1969, to August 11, 1971. He lived and worked in Miami, where he met his first wife. Together they had three children: Ericson, Kiamesha, and Christina. My father also had an older son that he fathered at the age of fourteen named Keith, who he did not get to raise. When the family of the mother found out that Stein had gotten the young girl pregnant, they moved her away and did not allow Stein to be in the child's life, fearing that his young age would prevent him from being a good father. After his first marriage ended, Stein met my mother, Elaine McMath, and the two later married on April 5, 1989, in Miami, Florida. They moved to Ozark, Alabama, in 1994 to escape the adversity in Liberty City, a rough neighborhood in Miami during the '80s and '90s, when they lived there. Elaine and Stein raised ten children between Miami and Ozark. Elaine worked as a clerk at Walmart and a church minister, and Stein as a mechanic and Sunday school teacher and deacon at the church owned by Elaine's mother. My parents had me on February 6, 1995. They raised me and my nine other siblings together before my dad died on July 6, 2006, from leukemia.

The Lee Lineage

Barbour County is a small, 905-square-mile county located in the southeast region of Alabama. Named after James Barbour of Orange County, Virginia, it was inhabited by Creek American Indians before it became a county on December 18, 1832. The fertile land was developed by Southern migrants as large cotton plantations dependent upon slave labor. With large concentrations of enslaved Africans in the area, the population was soon majority Black, a proportion that continued for decades. Twenty years ago, the median income for a household in Barbour County was $25,101. Today, almost 30 percent of the population lives below the poverty line. The population is still predominantly Black, as most of the descendants of enslaved persons still inhabit the area. When my mom moved me and my siblings to Barbour County in 2006, I never understood until I discovered my family history why everyone was my relative. Because my parents grew up in Liberty City, I always assumed that is where my family history started.

Louisville, Alabama, was the county seat of Barbour until the jail and courthouse could be built in Clayton. The first settlers of Louisville mostly came from North and South Carolina, Georgia, and Virginia. They were large slave owners like the Lewises, the Faulks, the Grubbs, McSwains, Pugh Williamses, McRaes, Shipmans, Burches, and Lees.

Violet Lee, born in 1825, was an enslaved person brought from South Carolina by her slave owners; she lived in Barbour County all her life, marrying her lifelong partner, Esquire Lee (born 1815)—a mulatto farmer who could read and write—once slavery ended on November 1, 1865. Violet and Esquire Lee are my third great-grandparents. The two had one daughter, Ella Lee, around 1854, ten years before the end of the American Civil War. The cause and date of the death of Violet and Esquire Lee are unknown.

The only way I could begin to understand the life my ancestors lived was through slave narratives. I would be lucky to find one spoken by my ancestors directly. However, I could only find narratives by their neighbors. In a piece titled "Slave Narratives: A Folk History of Slavery in the United States from Interviews with Former Slaves," I found the testimony of Molly Ammonds from Barbour County, who was owned by the Lee family as well. When asked in a 1937 interview about her life in slavery before the Civil War, Molly replied:

> "Well, honey, Massa Lee's place was 'bout three miles long an' two miles wide, and we raised cotton, cawn, 'taters and all sorts of vegetables. We had a mean oberseer dat always wanted to whup us, but massa wouldn't 'llow no whuppin'. Sometimes de massa whould ride over de place on a hoss, an' when he come up on de oberseer a-fussin' at a nigger, Massa say, 'Don't talk rough to dat nigger when he doin' de bes' he can.

> "My pappy had a little garden of his own back of his cabin, an' he raised some chickens for us to eat, an' we had aigs nearly ev'y mornin'.

> "De only work I done on de plantation was to nuss some little niggers when dere mammy an' pappy was in de fiel's. Twarn't hard.

> "Nawsuh! I ain't never seed no slave in chains. Massa Lee was a good man. He had a church built called de brush house, dat had a flo' and some seats, an' a top made outen pine boughs, an' massa's pa, Mr. Cato, would preach eve'y Sunday. We sung songs lak 'I Heered De Voice of Jesus Say,' an' I'se Gwine to Die no Mo.' We was all babtized in de creek, but none of us was taught to read or write.

"No-suh, I ain't never seed no slave run away. Us was treated fine. Our folks was quality. We had plenty som'n t'eat, but dem slaves hadda work powerful hard though. Atter dey come home fum de fiel's dey was so tired dat dey go raght to sleep, except when de massa had barbecues. Christmas was de big time; dere was several days to res' an' make merryin' an' lots of dem no count niggers got drunk.

"When us slaves was sick, Massa Lee would send to Eufaula to fetch Dr. Thornton to give us some medicine. We had de bes' treatment ever.

"Yassuh, white folks, dem days is long ago. All my chilluns done died or wandered away an' my ole man been dead goin' on twenty years. I been here a long time by myself."

"Aunt Molly," I interrupted. "There's one thing I've always been wanting to ask one of you ex-slaves, and that is: what you thought of people like Abraham Lincoln, Jefferson Davis and Booker T. Washington."

A puzzled expression came of the face of the old Negro. "White folks," she said after a moment's deliberation, "I don't believes I is had de pleasure of meetin' dem gent'mens."

When Rilla Lee was born in 1854 in Louisville, Alabama, her father, Esquire, was thirty-nine, and her mother, Violet, twenty-nine. Rilla, my great-great-great-grandmother, was identified as a mulatto woman who had between six and eight children and never learned how to read or write but after the death of her husband managed to run her own farm. In 1910, fifty-year-old widow Rilla Herring lived in Clayton, Alabama, a small town a few miles from Louisville, with her two daughters, Ella (twenty-seven) and Miltie (nineteen) and son Lewis (fifteen). Also in the household were her three grandchildren: Rosa Bell (twelve), Bessie (seven), and Grady (three), all listed as mulatto. One of Rilla's daughters, Ella Lee Herring, born in 1883, was conceived with a man named Joseph Herring, a farmer from Barbour County and a former enslaved person. She had many siblings and half-siblings. Ella lived in Barbour County her entire life and in 1910 moved in with her mother Rilla, along with her three children: Rosa Bell, Miltie, and Grady, who all worked the farmland.

Rosa Bell Lee, the daughter of Grady Lee Norton, is my great-grand-mother. Although I have never met Rosa Bell personally, I felt connected to her life the instant I saw her name on my computer screen, which was listed on one of the ancestry sites. I always said that if I were to have a daughter, I would name her Rose, with no middle name, to honor my mother and father who also did not have middle names. Rosa Bell was born in 1898 in Barbour County. My grandmother talked about her mother often. Rosa Bell Lee was a beautiful woman with long wavy hair that touched her lower back, which she wore in two braids. Her skin was high yellow with reddish undertones, and she had thin lips with a pointed nose and a keen sense of smell. Her soft voice matched her soft demeanor. Never one to argue, she would give her last to a stranger she passed on the street.

She married Willie Burks, who everyone called Papa Willie, on January 23, 1918, in her hometown. The two had fourteen children together, three of which died as infants. One of their children was my grandmother Rose Alice Burks. Rosa Bell later died in Louisville, Alabama, at the age of 51. I asked my mother and Auntie Linda why Rosa Bell died so young, and they said she died from a broken heart because of her relationship with Papa Willie. Papa Willie, unfortu-nately, was verbally abusive and had several children with other women while he and my great-grandmother were married. I also imagine that it was very difficult to bury three children. My mom tells me that Rosa Bell had to bury them in their backyard under a tree since all of her children were homebirths.

Rose Alice Burks, named after her mother, was born on June 15, 1932. Her father, Willie, had deep dark skin and stood about 5 foot 7. Rose Alice had her mother's soft hair and her father's skin and height.

My memories of my grandmother are a bit vague. When I was only seven, in the fall of 2002, she passed away. However, I will never for-get her essence. She moved slowly and cautiously always. She was very small-framed, and I remember her hands looking very similar to my mother's. I spent a lot of time around my grandmother because she and my mother were very close. My mom relied heavily on my grand-mother's support and vice versa. Rose Alice married a man named Reese (I was never sure if it was his first or last name), and she went by

"Rosie Reese" in her later years. Rose Alice was a small woman, with an immense presence. She would walk into a room, and people would immediately stop and watch her. My grandmother was a minister and owned the church, Holy Hill of Zion, in Barbour County that my mother would later take over. I spent most of my childhood in that church. It first served as my grandmother's home. My dad would later replace the three big cinder blocks that stood in for the front steps with a beautiful wooden porch and ramp for my cousin Tosha so she could get her wheelchair into the church with ease. It was a tiny congregation, mostly consisting of me and my nine siblings and two or three other families from the surrounding rural areas of Louisville, Clayton, and Texasville.

I don't remember my grandmother giving many sermons, because she became ill by the time I was old enough to remember church services. However, I distinctly recall Rose Alice's ability to minister to people who came to her, seeking guidance. Not only was she the lifeline of our family, but of her community as well. Everywhere she went, people were drawn to her, seeking help.

As I was continuing the research of my genealogy, I reached out to people whose DNA matched mine. One third or fourth cousin remembers her mom speaking very highly of my grandmother. Everyone knew Rose Alice. She never criticized anyone for their lifestyle and was always honest in her advice.

Magically, everything she spoke would come to pass. I remember one morning, scrambling around our house, trying to find my lost shoe. My dad was irritated, never liking for us to be late for school. In only a few minutes the bus would show up, and still no shoe. At that moment, the phone rang. "H- hello," I said through my tears and frustration.

It was my grandmother on the other end. "What's wrong, baby? Why are you crying?" My grandmother's voice was so soothing I immediately started to dry my eyes. "I can't find my shoe, Grandma, and I'm going to miss the bus. I don't want to get in trouble." I am sure she heard my dad yelling in the background for me to look harder as time drew nearer and nearer for the arrival of the bus. "Don't worry, baby. You'll find it soon."

"Okay, Grandma," I replied. I hung up the phone and with a sulk joined my dad to continue the search. In less than two minutes, there it was. I looked down, and my lost shoe was right there. *Why didn't I see it before?*

I never figured out why my grandmother called that morning, but I never forgot the sense I had after she spoke that I would find it, and after hanging up the phone, I immediately did. That would happen often. She could look at you and in a matter of seconds tell you all about your life. My grandmother was highly intuitive and spiritually inclined. She could speak about your future, and what she said would always happen the way she spoke it. My mother has that same gift, which I always thought was a superpower. In the African American culture, it is regarded as a gift of prophecy. Both my mother and grandmother were prophetesses in their church community.

Rose Alice had twelve children but tragically lost her firstborn, a baby girl. She raised eleven children, plus some of her grandchildren, including me, until the day of her death on September 27, 2002. My grandmother was sweet and sincere but experienced a lot of pain in her life. She watched her mother struggle with poverty and saw a man that hurt her often. Unintentionally, in marrying Reese, Rose Alice ended up taking a similar path.

My grandmother grew up in an old shack in Barbour County before moving to Miami in her early twenties. Since Rose Alice had so many children, she needed help taking care of them. She never had a steady job and never learned how to drive. She did not like the idea of being behind the steering wheel. One of the children Rose Alice gave birth to was Elaine McMath, the daughter of Mack McMath, whom everyone referred to as "Granddaddy Mack."

My mother, Elaine, was born on June 12, 1962, in Miami, Florida. She has high yellow skin, and her siblings often teased her about her complexion. "You're a White baby," they would taunt. "The doctors switched you at the hospital, and no one told you." Because of her bodily features, my mom looked very mature as a young girl—with long legs, wide hips, and beautiful full lips. She had the same presence as her mother. But she also had the height to go with that large presence. She was always the tallest among her peers and grew up to be six foot one. As a result, she got the nickname "Bigbird" from her siblings.

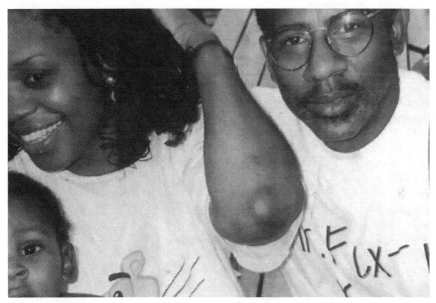

My parents, Elaine and Stein, in 1996 holding my younger brother, Elishua.

I always wanted to be underneath my mom, following her every step. She spoke with a sense of calmness, and I thought she was so beautiful. When she was six months pregnant with me, my mom moved to Alabama to be with her mother; she wanted to escape the lifestyle of Liberty City. During this time, my grandmother lived in the small town of Ozark, about thirty minutes from her birthplace in Barbour County. My mother met her in Ozark. That is where I was born and where my parents raised me and my nine siblings until we all moved away. Today, I only have two siblings living in the area. We remain very close as a family, even though miles apart. Our difficult past made us closer, and we talk every day.

My seven siblings with me (front left corner holding the eye drop bottle) after church in Barbour County, Alabama, in 1997. The youngest, Rachel, was not born, and the oldest, Linda, was living away from home.

After spending days researching my ancestry, I now had a greater appreciation for where I am in life. I am standing on the shoulders of those who went before. My brown skin is an indication of my past, but it makes me more secure in my identity, knowing exactly where and who I came from. Being a descendant of former enslaved Africans only makes me appreciate my resiliency a lot more.

However, there was a sense of transformation that occurred simultaneously. I found out that I had a great-aunt who once lived two miles from where I live now in New Haven, Connecticut, and I understood that feeling of nostalgia I got when I first moved here. My dad's family lived in New Haven and Waterbury, Connecticut, and I have been able to connect with distant cousins since finding this out. When I got to Connecticut, it had felt like I lived here before and that I was returning home because I had.

According to the great Albert Einstein, *"coincidences are God's way of staying anonymous."*

I truly believe that everything happens for a reason. Every incident in our life gets us even closer to the fullest expression of who we are meant to be. I wish I could tell you why bad and painful situations happen, but I do not have the answer for that. What I do know is that life is abundant, and no isolated event can keep us from enjoying the inexhaustible resources of this universe. The opportunity to grow from any situation is ever-present if you know where to look.

Do you know how the roots of redwood trees grow? They have a very unique and complex root system. Redwood trees are enormous; they grow as tall as a thirty-five-story building and come from seeds no bigger than the seed of a tomato. Despite the tree size, the roots grow only about six to twelve feet deep. They are able to stand so tall because their shallow roots intertwine with the roots of the other redwoods. They support each other. I think if humanity truly understood how connected we all are, we would learn a lot from these trees. We could all go further in life when we take advantage of the interconnectedness of our ancestry. We are all different but not separate.

Action Steps and Ideas Worth Noting:

1.   In order to know where you are going, it is first important to know where you have been.

2.   I encourage you to learn about your roots. This will help you understand more about your purpose and your interconnectedness with all of humanity. Start with your parents, and then find out about their parents. Ask questions and be prepared to receive the truth. You never know what you will find when you start digging but buried treasure may lie within your reach.

3.   Coincidences are God's way of staying anonymous. I truly believe that everything happens for a reason. Every incident in our life gets us even closer to the fullest expression of who we are meant to be.

4.   Do not ignore the signs in life or the moments that seem like a coincidence. Each moment is speaking to you if you are willing to listen.

Chapter 2

My Family Situation and Childhood Trauma

Bad things do happen, how I respond to them defines my character and the quality of my life. I can choose to sit in perpetual sadness, immobilized by the gravity of my loss, or I can choose to rise from the pain and treasure the most precious gift I have—life itself.

—Walter Anderson

Those poverty-ridden moments, growing up with 12 (nine siblings plus parents) people in a four-bedroom house, were some of the richest of my childhood. Obviously, I never enjoyed, when I asked my parents for money to buy snacks at school during breaks, that they did not have it. But they sheltered us from a lot of pain associated with a low-income neighborhood. The rock they used was love and faith. I was born and raised in Ozark, Alabama, a small town in southeast Alabama. As mentioned previously, I am the seventh-born of ten children, and mine was a very loving home. Growing up Southern Baptist, with both parents being ministers, meant we were in church for what felt like seven days a week nine hours a day. Unlike in, say, the Methodist Church, in the Southern Baptist Church, the congregation chooses its minister. As a deacon, my father often preached. And my mother, as a recognized prophetess, was a minister.

I will never forget the day we were having church service in my grandmother's church in Barbour County, Alabama, and had to start all over. I was only around five or six. My grandmother always dressed nice, wearing the most extravagant hats to Sunday service. My favorite hat of hers was this huge white one that draped over one eye and had white pearls around the base. It was beautiful, and she looked beautiful in it. My grandmother's church, as we called it, was her former home, remodeled to resemble a church, with the kitchen turned into a seating area and the front room the pulpit. A podium had been placed in the middle of the room, facing the pews. There was no central heating or cooling, and I remember the winter months being quite uncomfortable. There was an old heater that my dad put against the wall that all the children would sit around to keep warm. I will never forget the clicking sound it would make as my dad turned it on or the smell of fuel it gave off.

This particular Sunday, my dad was finishing up what felt like a thirty-hour sermon. Some in the congregation remarked about the absence of my grandmother, but everyone knew she would be there because she never missed a Sunday service. However, right as my dad was delivering the closing remarks, my grandmother walked through the door. When she and everyone else realized that she missed the sermon, my dad looked at the congregation and said, "It's okay. We will just have another service." And we did.

We had the same sermon again for my grandmother. I remember wanting to cry, I was so hungry. I was always hungry as a child because of my high metabolism. I was a stick and was often teased in school for my size.

My parents both had high-school diplomas, and my father attended some college courses, but they never had the chance to get a four-year higher education. I learned later in life that my dad received his real estate license in Miami, Florida, where he grew up; however, he worked as a mechanic at his friend's auto-repair shop during my childhood. He fixed cars and even spent several years remodeling an old Ford truck.

Without having much in terms of material abundance, we were very wealthy. My parents taught us the importance of family and love. Although I did not always appreciate being in church all the time, I now see that it was the best thing my parents could have given me. I was forced to go to church, but having faith was a choice. They raised their children to have a strong foundation in faith. My religious practices may have changed over time, but my spiritual faith has become even stronger as I work to develop a closer relationship with my Creator. No matter your religious beliefs, it is always important to have a thriving relationship with your Higher Self.

Your Higher Self is that intuition leading you to your Successful Self. Whether you call that Higher Self *Source, God, Allah, Creator, Most High*, etc., is up to you, depending on what makes you comfortable and speaks to your Truth. I like the saying from the *Tao Te Ching* that states: "The Tao that can be told is not the eternal Tao; the name that can be named is not the eternal name. The Nameless is the origin of Heaven and Earth; the Named is the mother of all things." If we could place a name on Infinite Source, it would cease to be infinite. Your personal relationship with your Higher Self will help you on your journey. You already know the way, but *you need to listen to the Silent Self in order to access that information.* This is why I recommend making mindfulness a part of your daily routine.

Research consistently illustrates the constructive relationship between mindfulness and physical and mental health. A survey of some of the most successful entrepreneurs revealed that they all meditated.[1] Meditation is a wealth habit. If prayer is you asking God for what you want, then meditation is you listening to God for the answer. If you do not allow time and space for the receiving, then you will always feel lost, thinking your prayers have gone unanswered. *If you listen closely enough, then you will discover that everything you need, you already possess.* Wisdom and understanding will help you unlock those aspects. I stopped praying for material things and started to ask my Creator for the wisdom to use the gifts already given to me to create and obtain everything I need. I started to realize that everything I needed was already here but me.

The Holy Bible, in my opinion, is the greatest blueprint and holder of basic laws and universal Truths. It lays out to us everything that is possible for life and the universal and spiritual laws that govern human existence through practical and spiritual means. For example, the Holy

Bible gives the greatest description of what love is: "Love is patient, love is kind. It does not envy, it does not boast, it is not proud. It is not rude, it is not self-seeking, it is not easily angered, it keeps no record of wrongs. Love does not delight in evil but rejoices with the truth" (1 Corinthians 13:1). Through faith, we know that anything that does not fit this description is not true love. The teachings of the Holy Bible also provide an elucidation of what our spirits are made of: "For God has not given us a spirit of fear, but of power, love, and self-control" (2 Timothy 1:7). I am not here to convert you, only to show you what has worked for me and to share my Truth with you. You must seek your Truth as well and share it with others.

There are certain events that undoubtedly and immediately change the trajectory of your life. When I was eleven, my father passed away from a rare form of leukemia prevalent among African American males. At that moment, I knew life would never be the same. I was forced to grow up very fast, and I experienced a pain and anger I did not know existed. Those negative emotions were the result of a lack of under-standing and the abandonment I felt. My dad was always active in our lives. He was a very quiet man, but when he spoke it was always insight-ful and stern. I remember him often lying in bed with one leg up and his right index finger on his temple, Malcolm X style. He was either doing one of three things: thinking with his eyes closed, reading a book, or watching *Seinfeld* or the Channel 4 news.

I will never forget the two white bookshelves in his room that tow-ered over me. I swore they touched the ceiling! Books about cars and religion, and a few self-help books, crowded onto the shelves, but on the bottom half of that bookshelf were what seemed to be hundreds of vinyl records. I was always so fascinated with the covers because the art was beautiful. I was a very clingy child for both my parents and undoubtedly a Daddy's girl. Everything about him fascinated me. My dad was in his late forties when I was born, and I always appreciated his salt and pepper hair and beard. I remember asking my dad one day if he would lose his hair and he said no. He was right. My dad kept a full head of thick, salt-and-pepper hair until his last day on earth, except for a brief moment in time when he went through chemotherapy.

Because of my father's love for music, he encouraged us all to play an instrument. Chopin was my dad's favorite composer, and he loved Michael Jackson. This resulted in a noisy home. My brother Omar, who played the drums, clarinet, and violin, constantly practiced in his room. My brother Victor played the saxophone and still plays pretty well today. My sister Tisha played the classical piano beautifully, and my dad loved listening to her. I did as well. I know that if my dad were still here, Tisha would have pursued a career in music and gotten into a top performing-arts school. He encouraged her to practice, showing appreciation for her talent.

My sisters Yolanda, Nika, April, and Rachel played clarinet (passing down the same instrument). My little brother Elishua taught himself how to read music and could successfully play any instrument he picked up. He even taught me the first half of *Moonlight Sonata* on piano. I was supposed to learn the flute. My dad was preparing me for it before he passed. I never learned, but I did discover an instrument that came naturally. My body. Learning how to dance, I could watch someone teach choreography and have it in minutes. I used my body to connect with the music. My dance instructors always seemed impressed with my ability to learn quickly. Besides the short piece of *Moonlight Sonata* my brother taught me and the two or three songs I learned on guitar in high school, I was the only one in the family to never play in a band. They used to pester me before I discovered my love for dance and how that connected me to music.

Think of the *movie Home Alone* or *Cheaper by the Dozen*. They closely reflect my life growing up with nine siblings. If we ever complained we were bored, my father would tell us to go practice music or go read a book. My parents both had a significant impact on how I navigate through life. I watched my mother take on several jobs to support her large family, and before my father's death, he taught me the value of education. And he loved me endlessly. I would sit on my dad's lap as he taught me how to write my letters and numbers. "Do it like this," he would tell me. "All you have to do is trace the outline I put of each letter, and pretty soon you'll be able to write it without my help." Such moments I will never forget.

I always wanted to be around my father, and he did not seem to mind. I love and miss our relationship until this day.

My father's death left a hole in our family that was never filled. I was very angry at him for a long time for leaving, but I did not realize until I got older that he could never leave me. I am a part of him, and his spirit will never leave me. It is never easy to talk about the time of his death. No matter how many years pass, I always become emotional, thinking about the pain he was experiencing during his final days on earth.

One day, my father took us to the public pool. Usually, he would bring his red swimming trunks so he could get in the water with us to teach us how to swim, but this particular day he did not. He was using a cane to walk, and I thought it was strange because not too long before that, my dad was taking me to the track at the Boys and Girls Club to run with him. He was also the same dad who randomly did dips on the piano bench. *"Why did he need a cane to get around now?"* I had known something was wrong, but as I watched my dad struggle to get comfortable on one of the pool chairs, it hit me that he was sicker than the adults wanted me to believe. I never; however, imagined he would not get better. We always got better after being sick with the flu or stomach bug.

I did not imagine my dad not making the same recovery. I can remember him becoming thinner and thinner, going from having a full head of thick, salt-and-pepper hair to not much hair at all. I asked my father one day why his hair was so short, and he chuckled and told me that he put the clippers too short but promised he would never cut his hair that short again. I found out later in life that he was going through chemotherapy. It wasn't until I got older that I realized I was actually watching my father die as he became more and more emaciated.

No one except my mother really knew how sick my father was. Being quiet, he was silent about his illness. When he went away to hospice before his passing, they just kept telling us he was sick—not that he was dying.

I cannot remember the last time I saw my dad. I had no idea the last time he went to the hospital that he was not coming home. I just knew I missed him during what felt like the two weeks he was gone until one day, everything came crashing down. It is difficult to forget. I slept in the room with my two sisters, April and Rachel, and I remember when I woke up one day, they were both gone.

The shining sun came through the east-facing window and woke me up. I thought it was strange that the room was empty, and the energy in the room definitely felt different that morning. What added to the strangeness was that the house was silent. Our house was never silent, but that day it was. I got up out of bed and dressed myself in a shirt I pulled out of the pile of clothes in the closet, which was a mix of my clothes and April and Rachel's clothes. Just like I did every morning, I headed to the front room, expecting to be met by one of my siblings who had gotten up early to watch television, but when I looked in the front room at this particular moment, it was filled with strangers. The adults in the room were friends and relatives of my father. I did not recognize them at the time because my dad's family lived in Miami, Florida, nine hours away from Ozark, Alabama. They did not visit often, but they were there that day. I wished that we were closer to my dad's side of the family, but distance made it difficult. The only children present were my siblings, but every other adult I did not know. *And why was it so silent?*

On the arm of our gray sofa, my mom sat, her expression obviously sad. My mom had very vibrant energy, especially when company was over, but not this day. She told me to sit down, and I sat next to my sister Tisha on the brown piano stool that was worn down from years of use. It always squeaked when someone sat on it. My mother took a deep breath, looked at her children, and said, "I have to tell you something that may be a little difficult to understand at first." She paused. "Your dad passed away last night."

After hearing that, I blanked. To my ears, her voice became muffled. It was like something out of a movie. Words stopped making sense as I stared at her mouth, trying to comprehend the statement.

Sitting there for what felt like thirty minutes, trying to listen to my mom but hearing the words, "your dad passed away last night" repeat over and over in my head caused me to get up and run to the backroom. There, I broke down. My sister came in behind me, but everything after that was a blur. My heart was broken for the first time in my life. The once-creative, happy, charismatic little Daddy's girl was gone with her father. I was traumatized.

At my father's funeral, I could not breathe. An uncomfortable lump sat in my throat the entire time, and I felt that I was going to pass out. There was nothing suffocating me but the feelings of anger, hurt, and betrayal. As we were led into the church, I stared at the ground because I was too afraid to look up at his casket. Maybe I thought the situation would become too real. "It's okay to look at him, baby," my mother told me as she marched us through the church doors with what strength she had.

I could not do it. I buried my face in my mother's black dress so that I did not have to look. When we finally made it to the front of the church, where his body was, I raised my eyes and was shocked to see him lying there. He had on my dad's clothes and his gold metal-framed glasses that he always wore but the man lying there looked so different. My mother wanted us to say a proper good-bye, but I resisted—still hurt and mostly scared. I did not understand what was going on. Everything was moving so quickly. Somehow my mom convinced me to give my dad a kiss good-bye. I was still frightened but leaned in hesitantly, kissing him on the cheek. I always kissed my dad on the lips before bed, but I still was not convinced the person lying there was my dad, so I kissed his cheek. He was so cold, and his cheek felt stiff. At that moment I knew for sure that was not him. My dad was never cold.

I wanted so badly for the entire thing to be a bad dream. I remember the whole day, the black dress I was wearing just like my sister's, my hair styled in two sleek ponytails twisted with bows on the end. I remember what the weather was like. Sunny and very warm.

I remember every single detail of that day. The green carpet on the church floor. The silk white lining of my dad's casket. The black limo that brought us from the church to the burial site in Barbour County and my little sister Rachel, who was seven years old at the time, staring out the limo's window as we drove. She looked just as confused and scared as I was… I remember it all. I tried to forget for many years, but I never will. Just from a single trigger, someone with PTSD can be put back in that environment. I cannot listen to TAPS without getting emotional. My dad was a Vietnam veteran, so they had the traditional military service at his burial. During the funeral, I sat in the very front row of the church, two houses down from us, that my dad attended every Sunday morning (before we drove thirty minutes to my grandmother's church for evening service).

I remember being held by my mother as the preacher, Pastor Boyd, who was also my dad's friend, gave the eulogy. He said, "Cancer may have taken the life of a friend, father, husband, and brother, but I will tell you what cancer cannot do . . ." I stopped listening as my eleven-year-old mind tried to find an association with cancer. It could not. I had never heard "cancer" before July 6, 2006, but at that moment I knew it was the reason my father was no longer in my life. So, I decided to never think of it again.

I admire my mother's strength. She lost her mother just four short years before the death of my father, and she tells me how difficult that time was. My grandmother had been her strength, babysitting us when both my parents were at work. My mom could not afford to be a stay-at-home parent.

When my dad got sick, he stopped working as a mechanic and helped out at home while my mom pitched in with more work. Watching my mother is where my determination and work ethic derive, including my sense of stubbornness when someone is trying to tell me something that goes against my Truth.

After my father's death, my mother's personality radically changed. She became sterner, unrecognizable to me. At that point, she seemed, to me, absent and at times mean.

When I was in high school, she remarried. That brought yet another personality shift. Our relationship worsened. We existed in extreme poverty. At one point we lived in a basement apartment infested with roaches because the people above us had them. No matter how much I cleaned or used roach spray, they were there. Having bugs in the house always bothered me because they were a constant reminder of the impoverished conditions we lived in. They would scatter across the kitchen floor at night when the lights were cut on, and I was always checking bags and backpacks to make sure they never got in. I hated them. I still do. Those were some of the darkest moments of my life.

As I think back, she too must have rued the day she was forced to live like that. But perhaps instead of getting even kinder, she was just too overloaded and went in the opposite direction. Absent. It was not until I graduated and went to college that our relationship started to recover. For reasons beyond her control, I was angry with my mother. I did not understand why she had not told us Dad was dying. In fact, after his death, we never even spoke about him being gone. I felt like we just pretended it did not happen. We never spoke about the trauma caused by his death.

I later understood better the full range of my mother's grief and the fact that she had to face everything largely by herself. She lost the love of her life and a father for her children but did not even have the luxury to grieve properly. There were five of us left in the house, but my mother still supported some of her children who had moved out. Within two years we changed homes a total of six times, and my mother worked constantly. There was a period in my childhood that I never saw my mother because by the time I was home from school she was at work and did not return until after we were asleep. In the beginning, she left food on the stove for us to eat after school, but that happened less frequently as time went on. It was during that time I had my first panic attack. It was in sixth grade and after the first time my mom moved me and my siblings.

My mom had bought a trailer in Barbour County, Alabama, for my grandmother before her death, and we moved into it to save money. Barbour County is even more rural than Ozark, where I was born. My family history traces back to that town when my ancestors were enslaved as mentioned previously.

One day at breakfast, I was doing my best to eat, but I was a picky eater and hated biscuits and gravy. However, it was the only thing available. As I sat there, going back and forth on why I had to finish my breakfast because I did not have money for a break snack, it happened out of nowhere. I did not know it was a panic attack. I just suddenly could not breathe, and I could not stop crying. It was not until years later, when I began studying for my first Master's in Human Development and Family Studies, that I learned when childhood trauma is not addressed, it manifests into adult mental illnesses, like anxiety and depression, and is also associated with panic attacks. In middle school was the beginning of my mental-health decline, which manifested as a lingering sadness that would not go away.

At school, starting in sixth and seventh grade, no one knew I was dealing with mild depression and anxiety. I was always smiling and laughing. I never wanted anyone to feel the sadness I carried daily. I later sought help after getting my degree because I was tired of my childhood trauma controlling my life. I wanted to be free of that hurt. Seeking therapy to help address the issues I felt powerless to fix on my own was the beginning of my healing process. Now, when I look back on my childhood, I feel love and appreciation instead of guilt and anger. I still feel sad when I think about how much I miss my dad, *but I am not sad*. I have peace in knowing I am blessed to have had the childhood I did. One filled with love and faith in God.

The four-bedroom public-housing apartment in Ozark, Alabama where my parents raised me and my nine siblings. Google Maps, Image capture, April 2013.

My childhood was a mixture between sweet and sour. Early on, I had everything I needed—two loving parents and a lot of brothers and sisters. All close. And we still are until this day. I can call on my siblings for anything and feel blessed, knowing I have their support. I hated never having money for book fairs or being too embarrassed to have friends over, because of our living conditions. I did not think we had a nice house, and it was infested with roaches. However, everyone always wanted to be at our home. There were a lot of us, and my parents were always bringing in more of my cousins during the summer months. There was never a dull moment.

Just after my father's death was the most painful, but we rebuilt, and my mother's strength trickled down to her children. My dad's presence—and absence—changed the course of my life. I knew that one day I would have the chance to turn that pain into purpose. Pursuing my passion for education would be my ticket out of poverty. I knew I needed college. But how to make that dream a reality? After all, no one in my family had gone to college, and my mom did not have the finances to send me. I knew that it was possible, but I was not sure how, so I started to ask around.

Action Steps and Ideas Worth Noting:

1. Childhood trauma is a common occurrence for many people. It can manifest itself in different forms of adult illnesses if not properly addressed.

2. At times, when the trauma is occurring, we may not know it. It took me twelve years to realize that the depression, anxiety, and panic attacks I dealt with as a teen and young adult were traceable back to the day I heard my mom say, "Your dad passed away last night."

3. Is it possible for you to trace issues that you deal with now, as a teen or adult, to a traumatic event as a child? Dr. Gabor Mate, a family-practice and palliative-care physician, has spent years studying the relationship between childhood trauma and adult health issues. He has dedicated his life to bringing awareness to the complex healing process of addressing a child's environment.

4. Start your healing process by addressing the trauma in your life. When you embark on that journey, it is okay to get help. You do not have to free yourself by yourself, but if you are scared to start because you do not want those emotions to surface, I can assure you that until it is done, it will be difficult to move forward emotionally and spiritually. There is freedom in healing. Life wants to open up to you.

Chapter 3

Against All Odds

You'll never find a better sparring partner than adversity.

—*Golda Meir*

My father was a very intelligent man and taught all of us to read and write before we started school. Saying that education was something no one could take away from you, he insistently praised us when we brought home good grades. He was very smart and could have gone to college but never did. My parents both had rough childhoods they were trying to heal from. Before she dropped out, my mother was attending a college in Tennessee on a track-and-field scholarship. She left school to help her older sister who was going through a difficult time and dealing with domestic violence, which left her suicidal.

By the time her sister was well enough, my mom had several children "out of wedlock." Eventually, she married, so she never returned to Tennessee. She told me one day that she has no regrets but wished she had finished school.

My father had more opportunity to attend school, and he did go to a few community colleges here and there but never completed a degree. I was not old enough to ask him why. My mom said that my dad procrastinated, even when she would beg him to go back. I do not know why my dad chose the opposite, but he was probably the most nontraditionally educated person I knew. He taught himself how to fix cars and read music, along with other skills just by reading books.

After his death, my interest in education peaked. The times when my dad taught me how to read and write and allowed me to count his money so that I could learn hands-on are my fondest memories. In those moments, I felt most connected to him.

I had always been a curious child and constantly in trouble for asking too many questions. I was not a straight-A student until middle school. I never made bad grades, but I was never in the gifted and talented programs, which in a way always bothered me because I knew I could be. I just was not focused. I would always joke around in class and never did my homework unless my dad made me. I was always in trouble in school because I was seeking the attention I rarely got at home.

I was bullied even more at my new school in Barbour County—not only about my weight but now I was being bullied about the way I spoke. They would say, "Why do you talk so White? Do you want to be White?" I did not understand what they meant. I spoke the way everyone else in my family did.

My father had not allowed us to use slang, and we had to use grammatically correct sentences or be corrected. Displaying intelligence is not an inherently White trait. Black excellence exists at all levels.

Children can be cruel, but my parents had lavished me with love and validation, so the bullying did not severely affect my self-esteem. At my new school, I formed a friendship with Gabby, a beautiful girl with dark brown skin I admired, and she was thin, just like me. She has a laugh that you never forget, one that instantly lightens the mood.

I remember one day in middle school when my attitude towards academics changed drastically. It was the seventh grade, and there was a math competition going on. At the end of the semester, the three students with the highest math grades would receive an award. I was not expecting to win because before then I was never a top-performing student. When the principal announced the top three, I was shocked to hear my name in first place. Students started clapping, and I heard someone whisper in the back of the classroom, "I didn't know she was smart." *I didn't know I was smart, either!* I won a $25 gift card to

American Eagle, with which I bought a gray sweater for $16. It was the first time I had that much money, and I will never forget how liberating it was to feel important during a time when I was experiencing so much hurt. I kept that gray sweater until I could not fit into it any longer.

My grades improved over middle school, and in high school, I was a straight-A student. I became less distracted, and my interest in learning deepened into a passion. Retrospectively, I suppose I did become a little addicted to the attention I attracted by being a top-performing student.

My mom eventually moved back to Ozark. At the time, I was entering the ninth grade and was now in the honor society. This meant a lot to me because I felt like the hard work had paid off. I was enrolled in advanced classes and loved every second of it. Not only was I doing better academically, but I made the track team and junior-varsity cheerleading team. I signed up for just about everything I could put my name on, including the U.S. Armed Forces Junior Reserve Officers Training Corps. I did not want to be home. Despite my mom's best efforts to find a good-paying job with a high school diploma, we were still struggling financially.

She eventually landed a management position at Ozark's Family Dollar, where she worked for over thirteen years. We were still trying to find decent housing and being home just reminded me of how much my life had changed since the death of my father. I wanted to stay at school, where I had more control over my emotions and attitude. My peers often commented on how they always saw me laughing and smiling—that I was rarely sad. But I hid my emotions, ashamed of my family's situation. I did not want anyone to know how much we were struggling.

As a cheerleader in my ninth-grade year, I met Brianna, the captain of the cheerleading team and one of the most athletic, popular students in the school. I admired everything about her. I realize now that I was so inspired by her because she was fearless. That is how I wanted to be. She would awe the crowd with a series of back handsprings, one after the other. We even made a game out of counting how many back handsprings she could do. Often, the crowd would join in and count the flips. She was amazing! A powerhouse!

The end of my freshman year was near. I had been so nervous to start high school, and just like that, the first year was over. I was still alive, but it did not take long for me to realize that high school was NOTHING like the high schools on TV. At least, my experience was not. I was very close with older students throughout high school and even now. For some reason, they seemed to have life more figured out than my peers. I gravitated towards their maturity and vice versa.

One day, there was talk circulating among the cheerleaders that Brianna had received a full-ride scholarship to any school in America she was accepted into. The scholarship was called the Bill and Melinda Gates Millennium Scholarship. It was a ten-year scholarship for disadvantaged high-school seniors who identified as a racial minority but showed "academic promise." As undergraduates, scholars were allowed to study any major, and Gates would cover it. However, as a graduate student, you had to go into one of the seven fields that were identified as needing a diverse presence: computer science, education, engineering, library science, mathematics, public health, or science (e.g., biology, chemistry, or physics). Graduate funding was also capped at around $40,000 per academic year depending on the scholar's location and chosen institution.

In my hometown, the ethnic breakdown was mostly split between maybe 60 percent White and 30 percent Black. The last 10 percent was a racial mix. I do not remember many Asians or Hispanics, or any other ethnic groups at the time. Brianna was one of the only Black girls on the varsity cheerleading team, and the fact that she was cheer captain may have stirred some unpleasant emotions from her counterparts. I was very quiet back when I started high school. I did not talk much, especially around older groups. I would just listen. However, a key part of this technique was to make it seem as if I were completely uninterested in the conversations surrounding me. I had perfected this skill as a little girl after being told repeatedly to "stay out of grown folks' business" or "stay in a child's place." I learned then that if I wanted to be a part of the conversation, I had to pretend I was uninterested—that I was focused on doing something else.

It was while being a junior varsity cheerleader that I had to use my valuable, acquired skill of pretending to be indifferent to ongoing conversations. We were preparing for one of our last pep rallies for the basketball season. Word had gotten out that Brianna received such a prestigious scholarship, but not everyone was happy for her. Some of the cheerleaders began talking about how they thought the scholarship was "unfair" and "racist." I could not understand how they were not happy for her.

Nevertheless, I approached Brianna some days later and asked her how she got the Gates Millennium Scholarship. She told me it was very competitive—she had to write nine essays to apply. Brianna also gave me a list of faculty members to go to for help if I decided to apply myself when I became a senior. At that moment, I decided to do everything in my power to make good grades and improve my writing so that I had a good chance of getting the Gates scholarship. I did not realize the significance of the conversation we had, but looking back, I can see how everything in my life shifted by this seemingly insignificant conversation.

Fast forward three years. I was entering the beginning of my senior year. A lot happened during my high-school journey, but those events were nothing like what I had waiting for me during my senior year. I was just like Brianna. I had worked hard to become a better athlete and cheerleader and was cheer captain my senior year. I was an improved tumbler, with some of the best jumps on the team. I found every opportunity to sign up for extracurricular activities and even ran for class president and won! Senior year was both rewarding and depressing. I kept to myself about the adversity at home, but it was no secret that I and my family were struggling.

I had had a crush since elementary school, on Eric (not his real name)—one of the tallest guys in our class—and I admired how intelligent he was. Eric was never the typical jock and not at all the class clown. In fact, he did not fit into any category. He did play sports and did really well in football because of his size and understanding of the game.

I never spoke to Eric before high school because I was too scared. I sat behind him in class because alphabetically his last name was right before mine. Many days, I wanted to tap him on his shoulder and start a conversation, but the fear of rejection froze me. There was also one major barrier I assumed would always separate us. Eric was White, and I was Black. Although that difference never bothered me, I thought for sure he would mind.

During our junior year, we competed on the track team together and became friends. Eric had a girlfriend who cheered with me, so I never wanted to cross the line. I never told him how I felt. Besides, we were from two different worlds. My mother would not allow me to date until I was eighteen anyway, so I knew the relationship could only go so far. However, I needed a close friend then, more than anything, and after speaking with Eric every day at track practice, I realized just how much I enjoyed our conversations.

That he had a girlfriend I cheered with made me hold back from any relationship of a romantic nature. I respected her a lot and later felt bad when, after they broke up, Eric and I started becoming closer. Eventually, the inevitable happened, and the summer before college started, we went on our first date. She was angry with me, and I understand why. I hated being a part of the reason she got hurt. I would have been hurt if the tables were turned (they later would be). Still, though, I would be off at college. I did not know where he would go. So, romance might be brewing, but for now, we held off.

I had no idea where to begin to look for university scholarships but remembered my conversation with Brianna. During the beginning of my senior year, I had a 4.1 GPA and was ranked number 5 out of the 200 students in my class. I did not have a great ACT score (standardized tests were a challenge for me), but I felt good because I knew I had put in the work all through high school to be the best student I could. Through JROTC and afterschool cheerleading volunteer work, I had accumulated over three hundred hours of community service. Cheerleaders had to perform community service after school on Thursdays. I was prepared to start applying for college. At least, I thought I was.

I had done the legwork. Now was the "easy part." All I had to do was apply. So, I began, but the only scholarship I knew I would apply for, for sure, was the Gates Millennium Scholarship. However, it was a very competitive scholarship. The Gates Foundation only chose one thousand applicants a year. The year I applied, there were over thirty thousand applicants.

I spent hours at the Dale County Public Library, the same one my father had often taken me and my siblings to when he was alive, applying for scholarships. From the guidance counselors, I would get recommendations for scholarships I could apply for. I went to teachers, coaches, whoever I felt could help me. I remember Googling "Scholarships for high-school seniors," and there were thousands. There were even scholarships for seniors who were cat lovers! I kept a journal of every scholarship I applied for. When I was rejected by one scholarship foundation, I applied for two more.

I was exhausted but determined. I never went out after school with friends my senior year, mostly because my mom was very strict, but I stayed committed to my dream. Your dream requires your commitment. I will tell you, although it may be uncomfortable in the beginning, you will never regret your commitment and persistence (unwavering faith) when going after your goals. Your belief in your goal is reflected in the work and action you take towards seeing that dream fulfilled.

Brianna told me that she had a teacher, Mrs. Juli Parrish, help her apply for the Gates Scholarship, so I went to her. Mrs. Parrish changed my life. I can never repay her for the countless hours she spent after school, helping me with my essays. My army instructor in the JROTC program helped me apply for a four-year Army ROTC scholarship as well. My grandmother used to say, "Closed mouths don't get fed." I realized exactly what she meant. You must ask for help. I had no other option.

Unfortunately, not everything ran smoothly. I had a guidance counselor who was not supportive of my vision. I went into her office one day, seeking help with scholarship applications and wondering if she could help me find ways to raise my standardized test scores.

"Ms. Letterman," I called from behind the red door that had a cut-out of an Eagle posted over the tiny glass window, "I don't mean to bother you again, but I was wondering if you were able to look into more scholarship opportunities for minority students." I walked into her office after being called in.

Ms. Letterman gazed at me from behind her desk and paused before responding. "Are you sure you want to go to the school you have on the top of your list, Crystal? Auburn University is competitive, and even if you do get in, you will have no way to pay for it because of your family's situation. You should consider a few of the local community colleges. It'll be a cheaper option, and you'll have a greater chance of getting in with your low ACT scores."

I looked at her, shocked, but agreed that I would consider the option if all else failed. That moment could have been discouraging, but I used it as fuel.

People will only show you *their* limitations. They have no idea what is possible for you. There is nothing wrong with attending a community college, but that was not my dream. My dream was Auburn. The hurtful part about what my guidance counselor told me was that I realized she did not believe in my vision and made me feel even worse by bringing up the financial constraints of my family, which I was very much aware of.

You must not lose faith when you know that you are pursuing a worthy goal. In his book *Think and Grow Rich*, Napoleon Hill states: "Whatever the mind can conceive and believe, it can achieve."[2]

By the end of the first term of my senior year, I had spent hours applying for over thirty scholarships—all at one time because I knew they were competitive, and I could not miss the opportunity for one scholarship while waiting on a response from others. I submitted my final application before the New Year 2013. When the spring semester rolled around, I was already getting rejection letters. A few. The feeling of rejection was gut-wrenching, but if I had not applied, the answer would have definitely been no. Then one day, my first acceptance came, and I remember the relief because at least I knew my hard work had paid off. In the end, I secured five scholarships, including the Bill and Melinda Gates Millennium scholarship and the Army ROTC scholarship, with over $670,000 in funding.

I will never forget the day I received the packed envelope for the Gates Scholarship. It came in the mail. I can remember the time of day it was. It was after school, and I was obsessed with checking the mailbox. I would check it every day after school because I was still waiting for my acceptance letter from Auburn University, which was the last letter I received from the three schools I applied to. I remember holding the letter from Gates, unopened, in my hand—thinking to myself, "Wow, I hope this is an acceptance letter because this is a really heavy letter for them to tell me that I did not receive the scholarship."

My intuition was right! The first word I saw was "Congratulations!" and I just lost it.

I did not make it through the entire packet, because I could not stop crying. I ran to my mom and showed her the letter, and we both began to cry. We knew that God had answered our prayers. My entire education would be paid for, including my doctorate if I chose to pursue it. I immediately contacted every teacher who had helped me and told them the news. They were ecstatic and said they knew I could do it all along.

The situation quickly accelerated when I got accepted into my dream school, Auburn University. There I was, wondering whether I would be admitted, and God allowed me to attend without paying a dime towards my tuition. I was walking through the very doors I once prayed would open. My family situation did not matter because your beginning does not determine your ending. Even if my guidance counselor did not believe in me, I believed in me and that mattered the most. I got a "full ride," which means the scholarship covered tuition and other costs of attendance.

That year, I was still cheering and competing in track. I qualified for State and became the fifth-fastest female hurdler in Alabama. In a tragic car accident that shook the whole town, I had lost my track coach the previous year. That day broke my heart. After my dad passed away, I wanted guidance from males. I never forgot that feeling of heartbreak when my dad died, and I would always say that I never wanted to be in love because I did not want a man to decide he could not love me anymore and leave. I was struggling with abandonment issues from what felt like my dad's disappearance. I stayed true to my promise, but I did seek male companionship from coaches and mentors. Coach Watters was one of those father figures.

He encouraged me to push past what I thought was impossible. His personality made it easy for me to believe everything he said about what was possible for me. The day Coach Watters died opened wounds that were barely healed. I felt like I had lost my father all over again and I was not okay for a very long time. I thought about him constantly and his two boys who were killed in the car with him. I dedicated my senior year in track to Coach Watters. I wanted to show him that I believed in myself.

My senior year of track was a success, leading me to qualify for a junior Olympic program called Down Under Sports, for which I traveled to Australia with other athletes from different states. It was my first time flying and my first time traveling that far from home. I was terrified but excited because I had finally raised enough money to sponsor my trip.

Going to Australia was exciting. For the first time, I did not feel restricted by anything. If I could travel to Australia by myself, then imagine all the other places I could go. Traveling and adventure were my biggest fantasies as a child. I never thought about my Prince Charming or dream wedding. I just wanted to see all the beauty and opportunities outside of Ozark, Alabama. I won Gold in Australia in the 100-meter hurdles, and so many people in my hometown were happy for me. I even made the local newspaper! The summer before college proved amazing for many reasons.

It was now the start of my freshman year of college. I had joined several groups, including walking onto the Auburn University track-and-field team, and I was completely lost. I was no longer a big fish in a small pond but a fish out of water. I had no sense of direction. I was majoring in chemistry and had a double minor in military science and Spanish, with hopes of becoming a surgeon. It had been my dream after reading *Gifted Hands: The Ben Carson Story*. I had written to Dr. Carson after reading it, asking him for words of advice for the senior class, and this is what he responded April 12, 2013:

> Crystal,
>
> Thank you for your letter. I would like to share the following advice with you and your class.
>
> First—develop a strong relationship with God. I firmly believe with "God all things are possible." My beliefs have served as a beacon of light in both my personal and professional life.

Second—surround yourself with positive role models. Look to those who have traveled the road before you; learn from their mistakes.

Finally—look for strength from within. I truly believe we all have the power to achieve greatness.

I wish you and your class the best of luck. I am confident that each of you will achieve great things.

Dr. Ben Carson, M.D.

Dr. Carson's words have stuck with me to this day. I was a part of the PLUS Foundation Scholarships at Auburn, a minority mentorship organization, and they put us in social groups based on our major. It was one of our first group meetings, so naturally, the leader had us play an icebreaker game. We had to pass around a beach ball with questions written on it in different colors. Whatever color your right thumb landed on was yours to answer. After a few rounds, the ball was thrown in my direction, so instinctively I reached out and caught it. My thumb landed on one of the red stripes that had the question, "If you could write a book about your life, what would the title be?" Without hesitation, I said *Against All Odds*. I knew then that statistically, I had beaten the odds. I knew that there was a Divine Source guiding me towards the path I was meant to me on. I let out a nervous chuckle and passed the ball on. It is funny how things work out in life. Now, I was trying to decide who and what I wanted to be as freshman year rolled along.

Action Steps and Ideas Worth Noting:

1. Turn your pain into purpose. Traumatic experiences in our life can either derail us or bring us closer to the issue we are destined to solve in this world.

2. You do not have to do everything on your own. Use whatever resources you have right now to put yourself closer to where you want to be in life.

3. Ask for help. In the words of my grandmother, "Closed mouths don't get fed."

4.   Plan for your future. If you have a goal, find out what it will require for you to accomplish that goal as soon as the idea comes to you. As you are planning for your future, tell yourself that it's possible. If it has been done before by someone else, then it is possible for you too.

5.   There are several ways for you to pay for school. If you are from a low-income background, then you have a greater chance of finding scholarships that will help you. Go to your guidance counselor and ask for a list of scholarships that other students have received in the past. After you do that, google "scholarships for high-school seniors." You will be surprised what you find. Keep a list of every scholarship that you apply for and hold on to all of your essays. You can often use similar essay responses for multiple scholarship applications.

6.   Dedicate yourself. If you want to beat the odds, then you must be dedicated to your mission and the vision you have for your life. Even if you seem strange to your peers, you have to do it. It will be a temporary sacrifice for a permanent victory.

Chapter 4

When I Grow Up

A man who works with his hands is a laborer; a man who works with his hands and his brain is a craftsman; but a man who works with his hands and his brain and his heart is an artist.

—*Louis Nizer*

As a kid, I always wanted to do something that allowed me to express my creativity. I can remember being asked, "What do you want to be when you grow up?" The earliest time was first grade. My peers responded with careers like doctor, lawyer, or astronaut. But honestly, I think adults liked hearing stuff like that, and children knew it. Me, I wanted to create beautiful works of art that made a lot of people happy.

I was very good at drawing and coloring as a child. I would compete and win school coloring contests, and my parents bought me art sets. Most importantly, my dad loved my art and always bought me notebooks where I could keep all my drawings. My career plans changed after someone said to me, "You're not going to make a lot of money as an artist," and that was the end of that dream.

You do not want to feel like a disappointment to adults when you are a child. At least, I did not. After that, I wanted to be a fashion designer or professional athlete, then a surgeon, and later a research scientist. Now my focus is on creating again, using my new skills. I just have a much bigger canvas to work with, and my education, both inside and outside the classroom, is my paintbrush. That is the mission I attach myself to: creating a more beautiful world by using my gifts.

By the time I made it to college, I had no idea what I wanted to be. Yet, there has always been an inner voice guiding me closer to my dreams. I followed my passion and what I knew would allow me to help people and provide service to humanity. As a freshman, I was studying chemistry with a minor in Spanish and Military Science with hopes of being a surgeon, just like Dr. Ben Carson. I thought since I was good at chemistry so far, I would be good at chemistry in college. I have never been more wrong. I ended up failing my first chemistry class. I had an A in the lab because I always understood things that I was able to do physically. I would spend hours in the library, studying. I never partied. I was dedicated to academics. I asked questions and thought I was doing everything I could to improve, but nothing helped.

I remember the day I received the grade for the last exam in my chemistry class. My class average was very low, but all I needed was a C on the final to receive a passing grade in the course. The class received their final grades, and when I looked at mine my heart dropped. There it was, a big "F" right at the top of the paper. I broke. I sat with my back against the wall in the chemistry building at Auburn and cried for a good thirty minutes. I felt like a failure. I had associated my self-worth with my grades for so long (being a 4.1 GPA high-school student) that the realization I failed a class hit harder than it should have. Fortunately, I was enrolled in a sociology course that semester, and I had a huge interest in that. I was gaining a better understanding of how the world worked and how certain human behavior could be studied.

I had learned during my first year in college that being inside the classroom was half the battle. In fact, for me, life outside the classroom is what made college so challenging. You had to learn how to balance life and classwork, and that was not always easy, especially as it was during my first year of college that things picked up with Eric. He ended up attending Auburn University as well. There, he walked onto the Auburn football team (trained with them) and later received a football scholarship at Auburn.

Although I never wanted to be in love because I was so afraid of that person leaving me, I could not resist Eric nor help but fall deeply for him. He reminded me of home. We ended up becoming even closer and eventually became a couple. We were both student-athletes, and he was a mechanical engineering major, so there were times we did not see each other for three to five days. However, we talked all the time. Our friendship blossomed into a healthy, functioning partnership, and we were happy together, but I still struggled academically as an underclassman.

Retrospectively, I realize that I had not developed proper study habits or time-management skills. And most importantly, I needed a mentor. I have never met any of my mentors—like Les Brown and Lisa Nichols. I watched their videos on YouTube constantly during difficult situations. Sometimes you need an outside source of motivation to help you when you cannot help yourself. I encourage you to seek out motivational videos on YouTube and find someone who resonates with you. Listen to them and learn from them.

Success leaves clues. They show you what helped them get to where they are. It does not matter if they have a more difficult goal than you. All that matters is that they were able to successfully fulfill their goals. One video I recommend is Les Brown's speech at the Georgia Dome, "It's Not Over Until You Win." Through passion and conviction, he moved the audience. I get something new from that video every time I watch it. It is important for you to know of others who have done the "impossible" so you can see that NOTHING is impossible. He states, "That dream that you're holding in your mind, IT'S POSSIBLE!" Your mind is wired to keep you safe, but it also keeps you from trying new things.[3]

I went back and forth about changing my major that semester, but I knew I would not be happy if I could not study something I was passionate about. I spent hours in the library, preparing for my chemistry class, and still failed. I realize now that I had gotten by so easily in high school without having to study that I never developed good studying habits. I figured that—to have more time for studying as a chemistry major—I could give up running track for Auburn and give up my ROTC scholarship. But I would not be happy. After talking with my older sister, a senior at Tuskegee University studying biology at the time, I decided what I had to do.

Telling me she wished she had changed her major as a freshman, she begged me to not make the same mistake. Looking back, I see it was the best decision I made as an undergraduate. On average, college students change their majors at least five times. I realized that I had nothing to be ashamed of.

Your academic strengths are important for you to realize early on. Sometimes they are established through trial and error, and sometimes they can be developed. I knew that I did not do well on exams. I have too much of an analytical mindset for multiple-choice tests, and my mind will come up with a reason why every choice could be a *possible* answer. I was, however, an exceptional writer.

I had more time to think when writing essays; I never felt the pressure of time. This helped reduce my test anxiety, allowing me to turn in quality work. Looking back, I had always been an outstanding writer, but I was always surprised by my perfect grades on written essays in grade school. I never believed then that I was a strong writer. My sociology class in college allowed me to write, and that is why I did better in that class than in my chemistry class that assessed knowledge through exams. Becoming aware of your academic strengths will help you succeed in college. You are not a failure if you change your major and adjust your studies to reflect your academic strengths. I am not saying to take the easy way out. There is no easy way out, honestly. If you are studying something that you are not passionate about, you will always be uncomfortable and unhappy. I am telling you to follow your heart.

If I had stuck with chemistry and quit ROTC and track, then I would have had an awful undergraduate experience. Who is to say that my chemistry grades would have improved, anyway? I most likely would have been an average student, still found it difficult to get a "practical" job after college, and would have struggled to get into medical school with below-average grades and standardized test scores. When you are passionate about what you study and it reflects your academic strengths, then you will go a lot further.

That is how I managed to go from a BA in Sociology at Auburn to a PhD in Public Health at Yale. I attached myself to the mission—serving others—and I was less concerned about how that mission would be accomplished. Possibilities present themselves to you, and doors will open when you are aligned with your mission. You become clear on your mission through self-awareness.

Undergraduate was a series of ups and downs. Because of my training in track and field, I always compare my life to running a race. The one I most commonly use is the 400-meter dash—one of the most challenging races. It is a mid-distance race that requires a great deal of skill and technique. You go one lap around the track, and you cannot sprint the 400; however, if you learn the technique behind this race, then you have a great chance at improving your time.

The first 100 meters is run strong. A good start out of the blocks will give you an advantage in the beginning. You maintain a strong pace at the 200-meter mark. The 300-meter mark is when you try to separate from the pack. A world-class sprinter accelerates to his or her maximum speed in 4.1 seconds. That speed can be attempted to be maintained after that. The object of the 400-meter dash is seeing who can maintain accelerated speed the longest and decelerate the slowest. Whoever does that wins the race.

You cannot coach the last 100 meters of the 400-meter dash. You just have to run. Exaggerate your stride and try not to quit as the finish line seems further and further away. I hated the 400-meter dash, but it was my best race. I had a long stride, allowing me to get around the track quickly with little technique.

I ran the 400 in high school and usually qualified for the state competition. When I got to college, however, I was performing at the bottom of the pack. The competition was more intense, and track became more about numbers than passion. Using the technique taught to me in college, I ran faster and better. The 400-meter dash still hurt no matter how much technique I developed. I felt as if a piece of my soul was left on the track after running the 400. It hurt to stand, and it hurt to sit for a good ten minutes after that race.

I ended up quitting the team after my third season because although I had improved significantly as a person and athlete, I knew that if I wanted to get into a great graduate program, I had to commit myself to my studies. I was a better student than an athlete and I understood that. You can become better at anything and develop any skill through repetition. Self-confidence is a byproduct of that repetition. You just have to decide what skills you are willing to develop and for what cause.

Track practice was Monday through Friday 2–5 p.m. I had all of my classes scheduled before then. No matter what I did to prepare, my stomach always hurt before practice. If you knew who Coach Rolle was and the intensity of his training, you would understand. He coaches Olympians and is the second-highest-paid SEC track coach. He was Bahamian, and his personality was every bit of that culture. I knew that, without a doubt, under his training, I would become a better athlete, but I also knew the process would be painful. Painful was an understatement.

This one day, Coach Rolle was in a great mood. That was usually a bad omen because a great mood for Coach Rolle meant a tough practice for us. It was also Friday, a day on which the workouts were more intense because we had Saturday and Sunday to recover. We did not talk or play around. Coach Rolle would scream in his Bahamian accent, "If you talkin', that mean you ain't runnin' hard enough!"

This particular Friday we had 200-meter repeats at 70 percent, which means that you put in 70 percent of the effort you would during a competition. Your 70 percent had to resemble that 70 percent Coach Rolle believed you to have, which meant that we had to run harder than we wanted. We did our warm-up drills, then made our way to the starting line for our repeats. Everyone began strong, but by the fifth repetition, we were hurting. There was no talking. All you could hear were the sharp breaths of every athlete as we struggled to stand and walk to the starting line again and again.

I had made it to my fifth rep, and by this time I could barely stand. Everything ached. The lactic buildup in my shins and calves was screaming for me to stop. When I got to the line the fifth time, I stopped and broke down in tears. I could hear Coach Rolle yell from across the track, "Let's go, Crystal! Why you stoppin'?" The more he yelled, the harder I cried because my body would not move.

Earlier that day, I had a tough encounter in the classroom, and I was already mentally drained. It usually did not matter how tough my days were before practice because I forgot about everything by the time practice started. That day was different, however. Everyone finished their workouts by the time I could muster up enough strength to stand. No matter how hard it was, I told myself I would never quit. I had always finished my track workouts since high school. That day was not going to be the first time I had not.

I remember getting to the white line, which was blurred by tears. The track was bright orange, so I told myself, *just stay on the track and finish*. I started to take the first step and found myself running again. I was probably running at about 40 percent at that moment, but I was giving it all I had. "Six," I told myself as I made it to the finish line. I was still crying and in even more pain by the time I made it to the line for my final repeat. I stood up, knees exceptionally bent because I was trying to keep from falling, and I took off. I gave even more effort on my final repeat and finished my workout at least 15 minutes after everyone else did. That did not matter to me. What mattered most was that I did not stop. That day I finished the toughest workout I had ever had. Most Friday workouts were tough, but I had never been that close to wanting to quit a workout. I have never felt my body and mind wanting to give up like they did that day. When I made it to the team room, Coach Rolle looked at me and asked, "Why you doin' all that cryin', Crystal?"

Why am I crying?!

I thought: *You are trying to kill us, and you watched me break down, and you still ask me that?!* No words came out when I opened my mouth. I just sobbed, and he dismissed me; he could not understand what I was saying, he said. That was understandable. What Coach Rolle did for me as a coach was more than I expected. He developed me, although through tough love. And now I tell myself, if I can survive Coach Rolle's workouts, then I can survive anything. I was never the same after that day. Initially, I was embarrassed because I was already one of the weakest links on the team, but when I showed up to practice the next day, I knew then that nothing would stop me from pursuing something I was passionate about and willing to improve in, even if it was painful. Coach Rolle just looked at me, and he understood the same thing. He told me years later that he always thought I was a hard worker. I valued the opinion of my coaches tremendously, so knowing that I was not a disappointment to him meant a lot.

Going through the Army ROTC program was a different experience. I never imagined myself in the army, but I do come from a military family. My army instructor in high school would always tell me, "You would make a fine officer in the army." Getting the ROTC scholarship helped me a lot in undergraduate, so I stuck with it. In college, ROTC was not hard, but the environment made it difficult to thrive.

I was one of two Black women in the program, and by my junior year, I was the only one left. There were three other minorities, but mostly everyone was White males. I was not sure if I was being treated differently because I was a woman or because I was Black. This intersectionality made it hard to be happy in the program. What added difficulty was that during my last year in the program, we got a new Primary Military Instructor, a Black woman with a successful military career. I was excited when I heard the news, but that excitement quickly faded as I got to know her. One of the other minorities in the program stated that she treated all the Black people in the program differently, and it was true. At first, I took it as her way of trying to develop us into better officers, but when she threatened to kick me out of the program because of my hair, my perception quickly changed.

At university, to make my hair easier to manage, I decided to loc it (in dreadlocks, but "locs" is the culturally appropriate term). My sister put my hair into coils so eventually, after a year, I could loc them. My hair grew just below my shoulders. I stopped using chemicals in my hair in high school because I wanted to improve the health of my hair and body. At the time that I loc'd my hair, military policy was changing the regulations to be more culturally inclusive. Black hair had been referred to as "unkempt," and I found this description particularly offensive.

The air force and marines had already changed their policy to allow Black women to keep their natural hair in the loc'd style, but the army was the slowest. I was hoping she, as a Black woman, would advocate with me to get the army to make the change sooner to match that of the other military branches. My hairstyle does not affect my ability to do my job, and going through that issue with her was another reason

I questioned my choice to join ROTC. I am not the type of person who insists on having my way. I do not have a rebellious streak towards authority, but I do speak up against injustices. I have found that when I do, people start speaking up against the injustices they notice as well. Sometimes all it takes is one person to stand up.

One day, she and I got into it about the style of my hair again. She wanted me to cut off my hair. I refused. My father never allowed us to cut our hair, not even our Barbie's hair. He believed that a women's hair was her glory (referenced from Biblical texts). It went against everything I believed in. I was emotionally exhausted from the ROTC program at Auburn. To make matters worse, the only person who could understand my position was threatening to get rid of me, so I quit.

Walking—though not storming—out of the building, my face heated with tears and frustration, I knew I was not coming back. I received a call that night from the administrative coordinator in the program, begging me to return. I had already decided I would just pay back the money the army spent on me up until that point, and that was that. Being in college was a positive for me, and Eric helped me a lot when it came to the mental health issues I was dealing with after my dad died. However, being in the ROTC program made things worse. It increased my anxiety and depression because I was in a place that made me feel inadequate. I was good at being an ROTC cadet, but I was not okay with being treated differently. I was a student-athlete while in ROTC as well, so I had to attend rigorous and intense track practices and still maintain early morning physical training standards. I was a top performer in the program athletically and academically, but other cadets would usually remark, "Let's go track star. I thought you could run faster than that," if I ever fell behind during one of our 5:00 AM workouts. I hated being called "track star" because I was not competing at the level I wanted to in track, and the tone used by those calling me that felt patronizing. I never spoke up about it though. I never spoke up for myself.

When I finally walked away from the program, I was choosing my mental health over a position in the military. However, one thing the administrator said made me reconsider. He said, "Harrell, listen. I know it is difficult for you to be in this program, but I need you to come back. No one can kick you out because I do the paperwork. We need more

Black women as officers, and to see you leave would be a disservice to yourself and others. Black girls need to see, through your example, that it's possible."

I did not give an answer at first, but I told him *I wouldn't allow someone to make me feel like I wasn't good enough. I was tired of being so miserable, so leaving the program was the only thing I could think of to restore my peace of mind.* I hung up the phone and prayed. I asked God to show me if this was the path to follow. I was confused because I was so unhappy; it seemed as if I could not win in that program. A week later I was back in ROTC. I decided that I would not cut my hair off as the PMI instructed, but I would comb out my locs. After two weeks and intense labor, my locs were out, and my hair was not cut bald. Less than a month later, the army changed its policy, allowing women of color to wear their natural hair in a loc'd style. They even removed the word "unkempt."

Now a commissioned officer, I see why I had to stay. The army helped me discover beautiful things about myself. I have since had several girls from my hometown and others contact me on social media, asking about taking a similar path.

Looking back, I am glad I did not allow someone's opinion of me to become my reality. I am now on my way to becoming a captain in the U.S. Army Medical Department, and I am grateful for the opportunity to serve as the first military officer in my family. New trails often present difficult terrain, but it is worth the journey. The riches you discover along the way will shape your character.

I graduated with my Bachelor of Arts in Sociology from Auburn in 2017 and was that same year commissioned into the Army Medical Department as a second lieutenant.

In my time at Auburn, I had been fortunate to connect with my mentor, Dr. Robert Bubb, who now helped me see that graduate school was an option. I had taken a strong interest in statistics, and I related really well with Dr. Bubb's teaching style in the Department of Human Development and Family Studies. He was passionate about the subject, and I could tell he was concerned with my success as a student. His class was the first moment in college where I had looked around and noticed that I did not see a lot of people who looked like me (students of color) and it bothered me. Auburn University is a predominantly White institution (PWI), so I suppose I should have expected that.

After class was over that first semester, Dr. Bubb reached out to me, inviting me to be his teaching assistant (TA). He said he was impressed by my performance and enthusiasm. I knew I had a lot on my plate with track, ROTC, dance, and trying to maintain a romantic relationship, but I agreed. I saw it as an opportunity to teach something I had great interest in, not knowing that I would be the one doing most of the learning. I did not realize how much being a statistics TA would change and shape my future. For three years, I served as a TA, and I loved every second. I was around the same age as the students, but as I stood there in front of the class, I realized they were putting a lot of trust in me. Every week when I got up to teach, I was nervous. With enthusiasm and my knees shaking, I would deliver the lecture. Connecting with the students was my favorite part of teaching. The professor made all of his TA's learn the names of the sixty students in the class, and I realized after reading *How to Win Friends and Influence People* by Dale Carnegie how important it was for me to develop that skill.

I knew I had a ten-year scholarship that (though capped) would help cover graduate-school costs. But I didn't even know what graduate school was. I had never seen that path for myself. In fact, I did not know what path was being laid out for me. I just knew I loved learning, and I wanted to help others while getting paid well enough to live comfortably.

Because of my involvement in research labs in his department, Dr. Bubb suggested I apply for the MS/PhD program within the Department of Human Development and Family Studies at Auburn—*his department*. I had no idea that the program was one of the top three schools for Human Development and Family Studies in the country. I just knew I did not want to stay at Auburn for another four years.

I wanted to move out of the South and live around people who were different from those I had grown up around. There was nothing wrong with those people. I just never felt like I fit in. I dreamed of travel and adventure. Marrying my high-school sweetheart within a few years of graduating to have kids and have them go to my same high school, never leaving the thirty-four square miles of Ozark, Alabama, did not sound very exciting. I was chasing a life of possibilities.

I applied for several graduate programs in social psychology—most in California—but I did not get accepted into a single one. Looking back, I know that I was not clear in my applications as to what I wanted to accomplish in graduate school. I did not know. I just wanted to keep learning and expanding the possibilities for my life. However, out of the seven schools I applied to, I got a call back from only one: the last on my list.

I remember receiving the phone call from the program director, informing me I was accepted into Auburn University's MS/PhD program for Human Development and Family Studies. I was meeting with one of my instructors in the ROTC building one evening when my phone began to ring. I looked down at the phone and saw that the number was coming from Auburn, Alabama. I do answer unknown calls, and at the time, I was expecting to receive unknown calls since I was applying to numerous graduate programs.

"Hello, I am looking for Crystal Harrell."

"This is her," I replied.

"Hi, Crystal. This is Anthony Bowman, and I am the program director for the Human Development and Family Studies program at Auburn. I hope that you are doing well, but I just wanted to call to inform you that you were one of the five applicants admitted into our department. Congratulations!"

We spoke for several minutes as Anthony detailed what to expect and what were the next steps I should take. When I hung up, I just cried.

I cried because that was the last place I wanted to be—I wanted to leave the South—but I knew by now, having received nothing but rejection letters from the schools I wanted to be in that were out of the state, it would be the only program I would be accepted into. I should have been happy at the honor of being admitted into such a competitive program, but I was not happy.

On the positive side, it flooded me with joy to think I could spend another year or so with Eric, while he finished his mechanical engineering degree at Auburn.

I still had some growing to do at Auburn. *I am very glad I got accepted.* Although I did struggle initially, I improved as a student by the time I finished my degree. I continued to teach statistics and developed better study habits. There were no exams, and I wrote more papers than I could count. I figured out I had a passion for research and that I wanted to study epidemiology.

Dr. Michael Kramer from the Emory School of Medicine was invited to Auburn to give a presentation on the relationship between slavery and the decline of heart disease in the United States. Dr. Kramer is a thin, middle-aged White male, with a long white beard and hipster aesthetic, who teaches about the Legacy of Slavery and how it still affects the health of Black Americans. I found it strange because I rarely heard of professors who aren't Black doing Black health research, and it shouldn't be that way.

Black health is an American issue, not a Black American issue. He was able to show that places with higher concentrations of enslaved persons in an 1860 census record were mapped to indicate a slower decline of heart disease in the US in 2016. Heart disease has been on a decline over the past decade, but at a slower rate in some areas. Those areas were where the descendants of formerly enslaved persons live. I saw then that he was using history to illustrate a picture of health in present society. I was noticing the connection between two subjects I was passionate about—history and health disparities. He made it very clear why Public Health efforts must focus on addressing the injustice of health inequities faced by people of color. During Dr. Kramer's seminar, my heart began to race out of enthusiasm. It was as if I had discovered a field of research that addressed every issue I was passionate about. I said to myself, "I don't know what public health is, but I want to spend the rest of my life studying in this field."

Auburn did not have a Public Health program, so I knew I had to leave to follow my passion. I was chasing the mission.

It was during my time in this Master of Science program that I discovered Black people were dying at a higher rate from a lot of preventable illnesses, compared to White Americans. All I could think about was my dad. I thought, "If we'd had more Black health advocacy and resources when my dad had gotten ill, then maybe he would have been able to get treatment sooner and still be here. I developed a sense of direction in that program, and that is the last tool Auburn wanted to equip me with.

After defending my master's thesis, *Socioeconomic Status and Health: The Protective Role of Religiosity among African Americans,* I did not stay in the program to continue my PhD. As mentioned, I knew I was not a good fit. I appreciated the mentorship of Dr. Bubb, and I loved the research. But I wasn't okay with just doing the research and letting it go to publication to "influence science," as my major professor at the time, Dr. Levy, so gracefully put it. I needed to see it through. Too many people were dying.

When you are searching for graduate programs, program fit should be your number one priority. It is already an intense process, with rigorous study. You do not want to make your time harder by being where you do not fit, or in a program that does not address all of your needs. Only apply to programs that you know you will be happy in if you were to get accepted. I cannot stress this point enough.

After completing my master's degree, I saw a path clearing. I applied for three graduate programs in Epidemiology in the pursuit of my doctorate *and was accepted into every program.* I assessed my previous applications and figured out how I could improve. I contacted graduate programs, making sure when my application came across their desk, they knew who I was. Most importantly, I got clearer on my mission and why graduate studies would help me fulfill it.

Being at Auburn developed my sense of self, making me realize I had what it took to be successful. By the end of 2018 through determination and A LOT of prayer, I had completed my first advanced degree a semester early and was on my way to George Washington University in Washington, DC to complete my Master of Public Health in Epidemiology. I wanted to develop a greater understanding of epidemiologic methods before starting my PhD in Public Health. Combined with my sociology and human-sciences degree, I was well on my way to becoming a Social Epidemiologist, just like Dr. Kramer, the man who expanded my idea of possibilities for my life.

So, what do I want to be? A creative—building and serving others so that I can leave this world better than I found it—painting a picture of possibilities for people like me. I want to continue to put my heart into everything I do and use my education to serve my community. That is the mission. That is what I attach myself to. Yes, my career goals may change, but I know that is okay. My mission will remain, but how I fulfill that mission is up to the opportunities that present themselves.

The truth is, no one really knows what they want to be when they "grow up." The people who seem to have life all figured out are just pretending, and any successful person will admit to you that they learn something new about themselves every day. Trust me, the journey of self-discovery is never-ending. That is the beauty of it. Otherwise, life would just be boring!

You are always changing and evolving. Always growing up. In fact, I remember having a conversation with an elderly woman in her late six-ties—a very successful army veteran. She told me that she still did not know what she wanted to do when she "grew up," even though she had already accomplished so much. I can say that keeping an open mind about your life and career is the best way to go. Always have a plan and have goals, but realize it is okay if they change along the way. Just adjust and keep climbing. Take with you the valuable skillsets you learn at each position in life. Knowing who you are will allow this mental image of the person you are meant to be to become more and more clear.

Action Steps and Ideas Worth Noting:

1.   Find a mentor. This is perhaps the most important piece of advice I can give you. If you cannot find a physical mentor, then there are many virtual ones. You never know what could happen. Les Brown was one of my first mentors, and just last week I had my first conversation with him in which I had the opportunity to share my story. On February 6, 2021 (my twenty-sixth birthday!), I was invited to be one of the twenty guest speakers at his Power Voice Summit. "It's possible!"

2.   Do not be afraid to put yourself out there to be guided. There are people who are more than willing to give you free advice if you ask for it.

3.   It is okay if your plans change for what you want to be in life. Follow your heart always, and you will never have to worry about not having enough money to support yourself. People pay money for what they find value in. When you have developed and educated yourself so well in an area, you cannot be ignored.

4.   Become clear on your academic strengths and weaknesses. Your academic strengths will aid you in figuring out how you can succeed in school, and being aware of your weaknesses will allow you to spend time developing them. There is no substitute for self-awareness.

5.   Sometimes people will see the greatness you have in your future and try to stop you. I cannot provide an explanation, but the best conclusion I have is that they are projecting their own fears and insecurities onto you. You must recognize when this is happening and act accordingly. Wish them well and continue on your destined path of greatness.

6.   Gaining clarity on who you are and what mission you want to accomplish in life will make your graduate applications stronger. Become passionate about what problem you want to solve in this world. That passion is undeniable.

7.   Put yourself in the path of your passions, and opportunities will present themselves to you that you never imagined. I knew that—even though I was accepted into the only program I did not want to be in—I loved being in school. Following my love for education led me to Dr. Michael Kramer, who led me to Public Health and my ultimate mission in life, which is to serve the communities similar to the one I was raised in through research and innovation. My first master's degree refined my goals and made my future graduate-school applications stronger. I learned time management, increasing my confidence as a graduate student after graduating with a 3.98/4.0 GPA.

Chapter 5

Make the Sacrifice

To be successful, you must be willing to do the things today others won't do in order to have the things to-morrow others won't have.

—Les Brown

You do not get something for nothing. You have to sacrifice a piece or all of your current identity to have the life you know you are capable of living. Every successful person knows that. What does it mean?

An example is given by one of my favorite entrepreneurs, Lisa Nichols. Lisa's story is the definition of "from rags to riches." She grew up in a rough area in Los Angeles and, despite her best efforts to escape the traps of poverty, became a single mother when her boyfriend was sent to prison. Lisa struggled for years to support herself and her son, Jelani, until one day she realized that to have her dream company, she had to make sacrifices. Her situation was so dire at this point, she could not afford to buy her son diapers. She was forced to wrap him in a towel until her next paycheck.

As Jelani lay there with the towel wrapped around him, Lisa, with tears in her eyes, placed her hand on his tiny chest and said, "Jelani, Mommy will never be this broke or broken again."

From that day forward, she sent a portion of her salary to her savings account. One she did not touch until years later. On the checks that she sent to the bank, she wrote, "Funding my dream." She sacrificed eating out. She lived with a roommate who smoked, so she put towels under her bedroom door to protect her and her son from the harmful secondhand smoke, and she never touched the money in her account for years. When Lisa arrived at the bank, she told them who she was and immediately drew a crowd. All of the bank tellers were yelling, "You're the funding-my-dream lady!" Lisa replied with slight confusion at their enthusiasm, "Yes . . . I am here to check my balance."

When the bank teller wrote down the account balance, Lisa did not believe it. She reported that the paper read: $62,000. After realizing that her sacrifices had paid off and that was, in fact, her money, Lisa looked down at Jelani. "Baby," she said, "things are going to be a lot different for you and Mommy." Jelanie replied, "Does this mean we can go to McDonalds now?"

I always laugh at the ending because of Jelani's innocence. He had no idea that that was the beginning of his mom's now multimillion-dollar company, Motivating the Masses. He was just tired of eating beanies and weenies.

Think about what you truly want in life. I need you to become very clear on this mental image because there are certain sacrifices attached to this dream that you may not be aware of. In high school, my goal was to attend college, but I knew my family could not afford to send me, so I decided to commit to that dream by spending hours after school applying for multiple scholarships. I knew I would need help in the process, so I went to teachers and even the assistant principal and asked for help. Was I intimidated at times? Definitely! Could they have told me they could not help me? Absolutely! But I knew that if I did not ask, then the answer was "no" by default.

You have to speak up for what you want because no one else can do that for you. Make your plans known to the people who can help you to get closer to your goal.

A few events in life will make you realize that everything that happened has led you closer to your purpose. I do not believe that there is only one possible path to your goals and ideal self—but that many paths lead to self-discovery. That is not to say you might not go down the wrong path. Many people do; however, I am simply implying that there is not just one right path. In retrospect, each choice I was forced into led to a series of different events, but what if I had made a different choice? Would I not have still made it to the same conclusion?

For example, after I finished my Master of Science at Auburn University, I always planned to attend Tulane University. However, after getting accepted into both Tulane and George Washington University, I chose GW at the last minute. I truly feel that if I had chosen Tulane, I would have still been successful in the program and completed my PhD in Public Health. I chose GW and ultimately will accomplish the same goal.

My advice would be to follow your gut. I had always heard that phrase, growing up, but I never knew what it meant or grasped the significance until I started journeying through higher education. I always listened to that inside voice that told me to go one way or another. There is a Bible verse I love that says: "Whether you turn to the right or the left, your ears will hear a voice behind you, saying, 'this is the way; walk in it'" (Isaiah 30:21). I reference this scripture often when I am trying to make a life decision.

I figured out early in life that when I did not listen to my Higher Self, I always regretted it. At that time, I had become close to the program director at Tulane, and during a campus visit, she told me, "If you decide you do not like it here, just leave. Nothing is really THAT permanent." Her words truly resonated with me and still do until this day.

The move to DC was enlightening but scary. I graduated in December 2018 with my Master of Science and started classes at GW for my Master of Public Health in January 2019. My winter break was not much of a break at all. In fact, it was one of the toughest moments of my life, but also the most significant—because I was finally able to do something I knew would push me beyond my comfort zone. Les Brown once said, "If you put yourself in a position where you have to stretch outside of your comfort zone, then you are forced to expand your consciousness."[4] I took a chance because I was seeking the freedom that comes with an expanded consciousness that all my mentors spoke of.

It was my first time living outside my home state, but I was ready. After my initial visit to DC a few months prior, I knew it would be the best place for me. Everything about this move felt right.

To feel better, I knew I had to find a way out of my current situation. My mental health was suffering in Auburn. I was just not a good fit in the program, and because I felt so different, I struggled to connect with my peers. My major professor (the head professor supervising my thesis committee), Dr. Levy, constantly tore me down by telling me it was impossible to write my master thesis in the time I allotted. I needed his support as a first-time graduate student, and I did not have it.

Also, my boyfriend (my first, remember) broke up with me as I was starting my last semester in graduate school at Auburn, precipitating the same abandonment feeling as when my father died. The decline of my mental health started with the death of my father at the age of eleven. But it had gone undetected. In middle school and high school, the issues became worse while I dealt with the adversities of home life and struggled to find myself. Once Eric and I started dating in college, I felt like I finally found someone who understood what I was going through. The pain of my childhood felt minuscule for the first time in my life while in my first relationship.

I took a chance on love, and it was a positive experience until things came crashing down. Upon graduating, Eric received a position with a construction company in North Carolina, but I would have to remain in Auburn another semester to finish my master's degree. He never asked me to come with him, and I knew he would not. The thing about being an ambitious, driven person dating another ambitious person is that neither of you is willing to compromise on your goals. Also, because of the love and respect Eric and I had for each other, that was never an option for our relationship.

Eric left Auburn and there I was, feeling abandoned. My biggest nightmare of having someone I love exit from my life was unfolding right before my eyes. We broke up because of the distance. He never wanted to try a long-distance relationship, but I did not want to lose him. The hardest part about that was, I knew it would happen.

Sometimes you really do get what you fear if you focus your energy there. I felt as if my childhood trauma was haunting me. Reminding me that I had been hurt before by a man and it would happen again if I did not face those fears. If you do not address your childhood trauma, it will manifest itself in your romantic relationships. I was only covering up my pain with a relationship and not dealing with it head-on until I was forced to.

In short, I was lonely after Eric left Auburn. I enjoy solitude; however, for the first time towards the end of my Master of Science, I felt lonely. I was hurting so badly emotionally and spiritually that when the time came to pack my apartment to move to DC, I could not do it.

I stared at the boxes flattened against the kitchen wall, and I could not move. I had stopped eating and would wake up most nights drenched in sweat and crying because of the nightmares I constantly had. I was not seeing a therapist, but I knew that when I got to DC, that would be the first thing on the agenda. I was tired of the pain of my past controlling every aspect of my life. I was tired of feeling so hurt and angry. Luckily, my mom drove an hour and forty-five minutes up U.S. Highway 29 to help me pack. I just looked on from the couch as she moved at the speed of light.

My mom was a professional packer, being familiar with moving. She did not let me touch anything. "Sit down, baby. I got this." I love my mom dearly and do not know what I would do without her support. Now that I was off at college, the ruffles in my and my mom's relationship had smoothed out. And we were in a good place. Looking back, I better understood how she had stiffened her spine and appeared to become cold in response to my father's death, finding herself at a fairly young age forced to finance the whole brood of us.

After she finished packing my entire apartment, she anointed my head with oil and prayed for me as I cried. I was so broken that I did not think I would ever feel okay again. For the second time in my life, my heart had been shattered by a man I loved.

Moving out to DC saved me. The only thing I took with me was what fit in my gray 2007 Hyundai Azera. Everything else in my apartment was either sold, donated, or thrown away. I cried as I stared at Alabama in my rearview mirror. I became emotional because I knew I was traveling outside my comfort zone, but endless opportunities for growth awaited me on my next adventure.

Sacrifices, by definition, are not easy to make. They are referred to as the act of giving up something that you especially want to keep, to get or do something else or to help someone. Dedicating my twenties to school life in order to pursue my doctorate was a sacrifice I knew I had to make if I wanted to do my part in helping to change the narrative of Black health through science and innovative research. Less than one percent of the population earns a doctorate, and an even smaller percentage are Black women. My education is not just for me. It is for the betterment of my community.

I never considered marrying and starting a family in my twenties. I have a lot of older siblings who are married with kids, so I see the reality of that lifestyle and its challenges. This door was only big enough for me to walk through. I could not try to carry a relationship with me, or a family, because I would have made it harder on myself than necessary. Even though so many mentors and professors were telling me that I was doing it "the right way," I still felt pressure to conform.

That pressure is normal, but you must remember your WHY. That will help you stay on course. If you work on yourself consistently and understand that *your path is for you*, you will go very far, recognizing the possibility of your dreams manifesting. It starts with the right mindset. Scripture states this point perfectly: "And be not conformed to this world: but be ye transformed by the renewing of your mind" (Romans 12:2).

Theodore Roosevelt stated that "comparison is the thief of all joy." Everyone is struggling with something you know nothing about. You could envy an aspect of their life and they are looking at you doing the same thing.

When you are appreciative of all you have, understanding that what is meant for you will be for you, then you do not have to worry about what others are doing. Use joy as your barometer of success. Are you happy with where you are and what you are doing? If the answer is yes, then you are on the right path. Remember, you glow differently when you are actually happy, so this is something you will not be able to lie to yourself or others about. Being aligned with your Divine Purpose brings joy and prosperity.

Ever since I was a little girl, I fantasized about travel, adventure, creating, and learning, and I am walking in that calling now. Everything will come at the right time, so when it is time for me to start a family, it will happen the way it was meant to. I do not heed society's standard for the "perfect age" to settle down. This is the only time in my life when I will be able to truly invest in myself and pour into my dream without having to take into consideration the opinion of a partner or child. I have true freedom to create and serve, and I am grateful for that.

The first few months away from home were the toughest. The biggest challenge was financial. I had received five academic scholarships. But they did not help here. All of them, except for Gates, were for undergraduate studies. Gates was the only scholarship that helped with graduate-school costs, but it was capped at around $40,000, far below the fees for attendance at GW. I did not have financial literacy as an undergraduate. So much of that money was spent. I bought a car and helped out at home with taking care of my little siblings.

The cost of living in Auburn had been a fraction of that in DC. I wanted to live downtown to walk to class and not have to spend hours commuting. I had no idea how to operate the metro, and it was time-consuming to deal with a paper ticket, so I avoided it. I would walk everywhere within two miles. In bad weather or if the destination was too far, then I would just drive.

I eventually got my dream apartment but not at my dream price. A few blocks down from the National Mall, I would jog to the White House to work out. I felt safe. As I lived next to so many federal buildings, I jogged past a security guard every five minutes. The streets were always clean, and as you walked a few blocks towards the Lincoln Memorial, you noticed all the tents set up by those seeking shelter in the city.

The apartment I lived in was ten stories high. I lived on the top floor. The floors were hardwood, and the windows stretched the length of the southeast-facing wall. From the rooftop, you could see the entire city, including the Washington Monument. Because I had to find income, I applied for a few jobs, landing a highly competitive position as an Academic Success Coach in the office of enrollment and retention at GW—becoming a certified coach, mentor, and tutor through the National Tutoring Association. I was making $20 an hour doing something I would have done for free, and I had. Helping students navigate through higher education was my passion.

I realized that many students just need guidance—sometimes just someone to point them in the right direction. I decided to use my story to help nontraditional students do well. I had asked enough questions and received great mentorship. I would spread that knowledge through my job and YouTube channel, whatever way I could get the information out. This book, however, will help me spread the word even more. *It can be done. There is a strategy behind being a successful student, and that strategy can be developed if you have the right tools.*

My first summer in DC forced me to work four jobs just to support myself. I was using the Gates Scholarship to pay the bulk of the $57,000 tuition, and it helped with the cost of living, but because the latter in DC was so high, I had to make up the rest. My first summer was a struggle, trying to establish financial stability while also adjusting to city life. Thankfully, I formed an amazing community of beautiful people through the GW Argentine Tango Club.

I threw myself into dance as an escape. I had danced my whole life, but tango was by far the hardest dance I had tried. Slightly harder than ballet, in tango, I had to release control as a follower. It was the only time in my life I felt I could not control the situation; when I did try to have control, the dance became chaotic, and my partner would tell me to "let go." *Why was this so hard for me?* With time, I became better and better.

When my Argentinian dance teacher observed me one day and said I could go pro with a few more years of intense practice, I briefly imagined dropping out of school and traveling the world as a professional dancer. However, school was my priority number one. Dance would always be waiting for me like a long-lost lover.

I began to thrive in DC! Having experienced my first Ted Talk (videos on YouTube I obsessively watched in high school), I felt as if my wildest dreams were coming true. I never thought it would truly be possible for me to have that inspirational experience. They exposed me to expansive minds like those I was now encountering in DC. I had also taken a personal tour of the US Capitol, and I often visited the free museums close to my apartment. I was dating again and conversed with intelligent, successful men—usually business owners, government workers, or lawyers. They took me to rooftop restaurants, where I saw some of the best views of the city. It was the first time I went on a date at a top-scale restaurant where the plates were a minimum of $100.

I love good food and good company, and I often had that. Dating in DC was easy because I enjoy a driven and self-reliant mindset, and most people there had that. I was always asking questions, always trying to learn, because I knew one day that I wanted to become a working professional and start my own business. I was surrounded by a wealth of knowledge and opportunity.

Most importantly, I became intentional about seeking help for my mental health. The panic attacks were persistent, so I was not fully okay mentally, which is how I met David, my licensed therapist, and a spiritual guide for me. Certain triggers in my environment would cause me to fall into a state of panic or brief depression. The anxiousness and panic I would feel usually came when I would try to control everything in my life.

Life in DC helped reduce the level of depression and anxiety I dealt with, but I knew I still had a lot of work to do if I wanted to be free of the anger and hurt that I had towards my father's death and later with Eric breaking up with me after he graduated college. Just experiencing the moment of the breakup, for instance, precipitated a panic attack. Eric was kind about it, but it naturally did not stop him from leaving.

Moving to DC was a great experience, but I was trying to rush the process of being settled into this new environment, which left me feeling powerless. As a point of clarification, the mild depression related to my childhood trauma felt more like extreme sadness at times. It usually left me crying myself to sleep (mostly in high school) and feeling as if being in a new place would make me happy (mostly in college). I struggled with being content with where I was in the present moment. I was always searching for that WHOLE feeling. Looking outside myself for happiness in a relationship or the next accomplishment. Never seeking the completeness in a place where it resided. Inside of me. In my own thinking.

I appreciated David's form of therapy because it focused on tapping into subconscious beliefs about myself and what was possible for me. David was also a hypnotherapist, specializing in Reiki. Reiki is a Japanese form of alternative medicine called energy healing. I had tried traditional therapy in the past, but I always felt like it was not getting to the root cause of my depression and anxiety.

David helped me clear my childhood trauma and was genuinely concerned with my well-being. I did not just feel like another client. He taught me ways to cope with stress, like deep breathing or the proper meditation techniques. We talked about everything! Spirituality, religion, pain, reality—there were honestly no limits, and he let me ask as many questions as I needed to. Walking away from his office felt liberating. Eventually, the depression and anxiety subsided as I gained a better understanding of what was going on internally, and I faced those issues directly. It was painful initially but allowing those feelings to resurface was helpful in the healing process. Dancing and therapy were healing avenues for me and helped me get closer to my Higher Self (God). I was beginning to understand who I was, and more importantly WHY I was.

DC was already giving me more than I imagined. The program was a perfect fit, and I loved the faculty. I made sure to research student reviews of faculty posted online. Also, I connected with so many friends. People who understood me and with whom I never had to apologize for any part of my personality. As an INFJ (someone with the Introverted, Intuitive, Feeling, and Judging personality traits), it can become difficult to form lasting friendships; it takes a while for me to let my guard down. INFJ's are referred to as Advocates and have a deep desire for authenticity and sincerity. Consequently, this personality type rarely settles for friendships of convenience. We desire a deep connection and will stay closed off if it is not present. INFJ's are less than 1% of the population and a few examples are Dr. Martin Luther King Jr. and Oprah Winfrey.

I can socialize easily, but only a few are able to occupy my space. Not everyone deserves to be that close to you, and that is okay. At the end of the day, you have to do what is best for your mental health.

I and my friends would meet up after class for happy hour and on Sundays for brunch. Happy Hour and Brunch were huge in DC, and I loved both. For the first time in my life, I felt like an adult. I felt free!

I was surrounded by people who had a similar mindset but simultaneously challenged the way I perceived the world. I was genuinely happy, and I just knew nothing could change that.

Life in DC was very good, but it moved so quickly. Fall semester came and went. After submitting my last graduate application for my PhD in Public Health programs, I was looking forward to starting the 2020 New Year, with a bang. I and two of my siblings traveled to NYC to see the ball drop—an amazing experience. We spent hours walking around New York and made it to Times Square thirty seconds before the big event. The crowd was lively, and I and my little sister, Rachel, rushed to make it through the gates.

Something comes over you that makes you want to yell at the top of your lungs as everyone in the crowd begins to count down, "ten, nine, eight, seven, six, five." The excitement grew louder: "four, three, two, one! Happy New Year!" I was overwhelmed with emotion. 2020 had begun. 2019 was a great year, and I expected nothing less from 2020. I had started my healing journey and was looking forward to the strides I would make in the year to come. I had my twenty-fifth birthday that next month and celebrated with my siblings in Atlanta. We were all together again, and it felt great.

That same month I found out I was invited to Yale for an interview for their PhD in Public Health program. I could not believe it! I almost did not apply to Yale because I did not believe I would get in due to my low Graduate Record Exam (GRE) scores. GRE is a multiple-choice, computer-based program to test analytical, verbal, and quantitative reasoning, but my advisor at GW, Dr. Magnus, encouraged me to apply. I went into her office one day, extremely discouraged because I knew I wanted to continue the religious/spiritual-based research I had started, but the professors doing that research were at Harvard and Yale.

I sat in her office as my eyes swelled up with tears, explaining to her how I did not want to give up my research focus, but I knew I would have to apply to very competitive schools if I wanted to work with some of the top researchers in the field who specialized in that area of research. She looked at me from behind her desk and said one word I will never forget, "So." I repeated what I'd just said because I was unsure if she heard the names of the schools. She waited a moment and said,

"You already have so many things going against you. You already have so many people trying to count you out. Don't count yourself out."

This is why I say it is important to research your prospective programs and consider faculty reviews. GW had the highest reviews out of all the MPH programs I was accepted into, and I saw why.

Dr. Magnus changed my life. If it were not for her words then, I might not have applied to Yale at all. She helped me see that *I was the only one standing in my way*. The interviews at Yale were intense. I was nervous, but I led each interview with my passion. I had connected in advance with the professor specializing in religious/spiritual-based research at Yale, and when I got there he said, "The faculty were waiting to meet you." I had not been shy about reaching out to Yale admissions every chance I got. I called to make sure they would accept my GRE scores. As I already explained, I did poorly on this kind of test, always second thinking possible exceptions and alternate analyses—hallmarks, I later discovered, of a creative mind.

I also called Yale before applying, to learn more about the program and advice on what would make me a competitive applicant for their school. I emailed faculty constantly, and they were all so responsive. By the time I made it there to interview, they only needed to put a face with the name.

Being in the Yale School of Public Health felt right. I cannot really explain it, but I felt like I belonged, which was a surprise to me because I thought for sure I would feel out of place. Not a single person I knew had been accepted into an Ivy League institution. Why would they want me?

I did not know what to expect. I was still insecure because of my low test scores and nontraditional background. Those programs were highly competitive, and I had received an interview for the PhD programs at GW and Hopkins as well, but I did not get an acceptance letter from them. I was even rejected from UCLA because of my test scores. I know because after being rejected, I called them and asked why I did not get into their doctoral program.

It was a Wednesday evening. I had just got back to my 550-square-foot studio apartment in downtown DC. Wednesdays were always my longest days. I was beat. As I lay there on my bed, staring out the window at the night sky, I felt a buzz from my cell phone. So reluctantly, I checked my email. The first thing I saw was "Congratulations!" When I opened the email it read:

> Dear Crystal,
>
> I hope this email finds you well. I am extremely pleased to let you know that you have been admitted to the Yale School of Public Health PhD program. Your visit last week totally convinced our faculty that you would be an excellent addition to our program. In recognition of your outstanding accomplishments and exceptional promise, you will receive a Yale School of Public Health Research Award of $2,000.
>
> I recognize that choosing a graduate program can be overwhelming and thus, I am available to answer any questions about our program.
>
> Congratulations and my very best wishes.
>
> David

I immediately screamed! Just to make sure I was reading what I thought I was reading, I read the email over and over again. "Choosing a graduate program?!" I thought, "I will accept this very second! What do I have to think about? It's Yale!" I didn't, though. I told myself that I had to calm down, get some rest, and in the morning reread the email to make sure I read it correctly and that I wasn't just making it all up in my head. For the next hour, I sat in my bed and screamed into my pillow over and over, "YALE?! Seriously, Yale?!" I thanked God and cried myself to sleep, so overwhelmed with emotion, both positive and negative. I felt guilty because I didn't understand how something this amazing could happen to me, but grateful because it did.

The program was fully funded plus a graduate stipend of $36,000. The $2,000 was on top of that and is typically used for books and supplies. The next morning, I called my mom and told her the news, and we both thanked God together, just like we did when I had received the Bill Gates Scholarship seven years prior. I felt like I had received the golden ticket both times. And both times it was a result of God's grace. But the beautiful thing about His grace is that it covers all of us.

Next, I called everyone who wrote a letter of recommendation for me. My dean from Auburn, whom I loved because he helped me out of so many situations, and when I graduated with my Bachelor of Arts, he gave me a hug as I walked across the graduating stage instead of a handshake, like everyone else. It made me feel like he truly did have my best interests at heart. I called my mentor and former statistics professor, Dr. Bubb, who has guided me through most of graduate school. He was the first to encourage me to consider applying to grad school, even though I had no idea what it was at the time. I also called my mentor from the Gates Foundation and my advisor from GW, Dr. Magnus. It really does take a village because I would not have gotten there on my own.

News spread around my hometown fast, and the family all supported me. My cousin texted me, "Uncle Stein would be so proud of you." I paused, then thanked her. I missed my dad greatly and always imagined what he would have thought to see one of his baby girls accepted into Yale. I bet he saw that possibility for me long before I did, and that is why he always encouraged me to learn as much as I could and do well in school. My education is for me. It is the tool I use to serve others, but I have dedicated it to my father and the legacy he left.

I mentioned earlier that when I was little, I had always wanted to be an artist. I spent hours drawing, creating new things. I can remember using shoe boxes, beads that my mom would put in our hair, and other little items from around the house to build models of my dream bedroom or bedrooms for my dolls. I had six sisters and three brothers in the house with me, so I never had my own room. I didn't have my own room until I was a junior in college. I imagined having a space to call my own, where I would hang my art and finally enjoy that pink-and-green color scheme I'd always wanted.

I never thought I would want to be a research scientist, though. How could a little girl growing up in public housing in rural Alabama know what a research scientist was? However, I have always asked a lot of questions. One day, when I was a first-grade student, my teacher was explaining to the class how we were to perform a task for a project; however, I became really eager and would ask questions as soon as they arose in my head. After my third or fourth time asking a question, Mrs. Thompson became frustrated. "Go to the corner, Crystal," my teacher shouted, "I was just about to explain that!"

As you can imagine, I was terribly embarrassed. There is only one thing I hated more than being scolded as a child, and that was being scolded in front of other people. My tears ran hot down my cheeks as—frustrated and ashamed—I stood in the corner.

I love research. I have always loved finding out the "how" and "why," I am not surprised that I came to want to be a research scientist. Like an artist, I start with a vision and put pieces together to see that vision manifested in physical form. Instead of creating my dream room, I am creating my dreamworld. One in which hearing the words "You have cancer" does not feel like a death sentence. And a place where social constructs like race and gender do not determine the lifespan or lifestyle of an individual. We all deserve an equal chance at a full life, I believe in health equity because the people before me believed in equality for all and fought for it. In the words of the late Dr. Martin Luther King, Jr., "Of all the forms of inequality, injustice in health care is the most shocking and inhumane."

Action Steps and Ideas Worth Noting:

1.   Every successful person knows that you do not get something for nothing. You have to sacrifice a piece or all of your current identity to have the life you know you are capable of living.

2.   It is okay to take calculated risks. Follow your gut.

3.   Do not compare yourself to your peers, thinking they seem to have it figured out. There's a good chance they don't. Not yet. Stay true to yourself and follow your own path.

4.   Choosing to delay making a sacrifice because you fear it will be difficult will only further complicate your mission. As Les Brown often states, "If you do what is easy, your life will be hard. If you do what is hard, then your life will be easy."[5] Do the hard stuff now, and you will enjoy freedom much sooner in life.

5.   Sometimes difficult situations come to mold you and shape you into the person you were always meant to be. Moving away from home was difficult at first, but I eventually established myself in a new environment. That new environment brought countless opportunities. You've heard the saying, "A comfort zone is a beautiful place, but nothing ever grows there."[6] You will discover different aspects of your character when your limits on what is possible for you are challenged.

6.   Test scores do not determine your worth as a student. If you are aiming for competitive programs, then highlight your academic strengths in your applications. Your passion will put you in the places you are meant to be if you are clear on your goals.

Chapter 6

The Value of a Dream

Those times when you get up early and you work hard, those times when you stay up late and you work hard, those times when you don't feel like working, you're too tired, you don't want to push yourself, but you do it anyway. That is actually the dream. That's the dream. It's not the destination, it's the journey.

—Kobe Bryant

During the process of applying for scholarships in my senior year of high school, I had to write myriad essays on varied topics. But the admissions departments were all aiming to find out why they should invest in me. Essentially, what made ME worth their money? I do not remember exactly which scholarship it was, but one of the questions was to write about the best advice I ever received. I remember this essay because it sparked an emotion in me I will never forget. After reading the prompt, without hesitation, I wrote, "The best advice I have ever received was to follow my dreams . . ." Maybe I knew subconsciously that was the advice I would carry with me throughout my entire journey.

Some people know in childhood exactly what they want to do, and they follow through into adulthood. However, if you are like me and so many others, you end up following a path different than the one you originally thought best. I have always gravitated towards older individuals in my life, for some reason—as if they were superhumans with a wealth of knowledge. They are also funny and more themselves than any other group I have met. During graduate school at George Washington University, I met so many professors who had an array of experiences in subjects ranging from medical school and chemistry to engineering. After reading *Becoming* by Michelle Obama and learning about the different career paths she took, I realized it was normal to have various interests. Having that diverse background is an asset. In the words of Vincent van Gogh in his letters, "Those who love much, do much and accomplish much, and whatever is done with love is done well."[7]

I want you to think about your dream. KNOW that it's possible. Knowing goes beyond belief. Every decision that I have ever made in life has been backed by an internal urge. Every time I followed that urge, a door, or multiple doors, opened. That is not to say I did not experience adversity. In fact, adversity was waiting on the other side of most of those doors.

In retrospect, those challenges were there to develop me. I was not meant to walk through each door in the same mindset. My mind had to become developed along the way so that I was able to handle the manifestation of my dreams. From experience, I know that the mind is where all the battles in life take place. There is a saying by wealth coach James Mel that I like that goes, "90 percent of the game is played above the shoulders."[8] It is where victories take place as well.

There is an African proverb that also resonates with me that states, "When there is no enemy within, the enemies outside cannot harm you."

The first place you lose the battle is in your mind. You must realize the power of your mind. I would encourage you to read books on how to change your thinking to more positive patterns. Patterns that serve you and your Divine Purpose.

I learned during my early developing stages that everything in life wants to keep moving forward—that is, expanding. The universe and everything in it (including you) is lifeward. That means that no matter how far you go in life, no matter what you accomplish, your Higher Self will always want to keep growing, expanding. When you stop growing and feel that you have done enough learning, that is a cue to become dissatisfied, that is the beginning of spiritual death. When I moved from Alabama, I thought I was at the best point in life I could be. My dream had been to move out of the South and be surrounded by people I bonded with—people who thought differently than what I was accustomed to. Moving from small-town Ozark, Alabama, to Washington, DC, was more than just a dream come true. It was the catalyst for my journey to self-discovery. It was the start of my healing process.

In my head, I thought I would go to George Washington University and finish out my PhD. Afterward, I would begin work as a research scientist with the Centers for Disease Control and Prevention, and that would be my story. I would feel complete and content and not develop any new dreams or goals, because I had already accomplished my ultimate dream. Wrong!!!

There is no "ultimate dream." If I am living on this earth, I will always have dreams and goals, and I am okay with that. At the end of my life, I want to say that I used every gift God gave me. Dr. Myles Munroe once said that the graveyard is the richest place on earth. There, you find books that were never written, songs that were never composed, and businesses that never left the ground. I want to say that I never settled or compromised on my dreams. I have heard so many people say later in life they regret not following their dreams. Sarah Bombell stated, "The pain of discipline is far less than the pain of regret." If pain in this life is inevitable, I would rather deal with the pain of growth versus the pain of regret. Growing pains are only temporary; the latter is not.

Moving to Washington, DC was a dream come true for me. However, I underestimated the amount of change. There was no such thing there as the "Southern hospitality" I was so used to, and I was taken aback by the cost of living. In fact, I had a panic attack while driving back to my apartment one day, because it started snowing and I ended up missing my exit twice on the interstate. That moment, I now see, was a trigger for me. I didn't realize it at the time, but I truly missed home. I missed my comfort zone. I missed small things I never noticed before.

When I was in the MS/PhD program at Auburn, although comfortable, I was completely miserable, knowing I would not develop there at the level I could, had I just been somewhere that did not make me feel so content, but rather challenged me. I was ready to experience a bigger city like I had always dreamed of. Looking back, I can see that I added to my misery by not being patient. I would promise myself, *just graduate with your first master's degree, move to DC, and then you will be happy*. However, when I graduated, I was not happy. I knew then that my joy did not hinge on any accomplishment.

In DC, I definitely stepped outside of my comfort zone. I will caution you—when you decide to take a leap of faith toward following your dreams—to be aware of the changes going on in your life. The universe will be on your side; however, that does not remove the turbulence. Understand that that turbulence is a part of your journey, a step toward your dream. It is okay to not feel comfortable during this time of growth. Remember why you decided to go after your dream in the first place, and that will carry you. Know that there is something inside of you that is greater than any obstacle.

No one told me that the changes I would experience after moving to a new city would cause me to panic or question who I was. There were points where I did not recognize myself. I knew that there was no going back to my old habits of thinking. The direction my life was going in required me to have a certain type of mental agility. Looking back, I guess I should have expected it. Nonetheless, it happened, and I am better and stronger because I realized then that I could do anything I put my mind to and live anywhere I wanted to. Eventually, I would adjust to any change that presented itself in my life. That is what we do as human beings. We adapt and survive.

I challenge you to not only survive but also THRIVE. Your dreams were given to you for a reason, not just by chance. Go after that dream with unfailing faith that you will be successful. I learned that the easiest thing I ever did was follow my dreams, but the hardest thing I ever did was believe I was worthy enough to have my heart's desires. Belief is what got me this far, and belief in myself and the God in me is what will take me even further. You are the only one who can determine your success or failure. Do not count yourself out. Do not be the only one standing in your way. In the words of Eleanor Roosevelt, "The future belongs to those who believe in the beauty of their dreams."[9]

Action Steps and Ideas Worth Noting:

1.   What is your dream? What is the one thing you would like to accomplish if you knew that failing wasn't a possibility? As you are holding that dream in your mind, please know that it's possible. That is all you need to know.

2.   Are you currently living out your dreams or are you operating out of a place of fear? Use joy as a barometer? Joy will tell you if you are truly living the life you know you are capable of.

3.   Use your imagination to create the life of your dreams and write them down. Develop an unwavering sense of belief that it's possible for you to accomplish whatever goal you set your mind to. Yes, it will take hard work and dedication. However, struggling is optional. Learn from those who have gone before you to minimize the struggle.

4.   Develop yourself and your dream through self-awareness. You get this awareness through education. Educate yourself inside and outside of the classroom. There is no substitute for self-awareness.

Chapter 7

The Promised Land

Resolve to be thyself; and know that he who finds himself, loses his misery.

—Matthew Arnold

At the time I received my acceptance letter to Yale, I still had not developed the best self-esteem. I found myself imagining scenarios where I would receive an email from Yale saying they got my application mixed up with another student's or something along the lines of, "Dear Crystal, we are sorry to inform you but upon further review of your application, we have decided that your scores are too low despite your academic ability, and you can't come to our school. Sorry."

It took me an entire week to announce my acceptance to Yale on social media because I was so afraid that they were going to take it back.

To make matters worse, around the time I was being invited back to Yale for a second look when they took accepted students around the city and helped them find an apartment, COVID hit, and the entire world shut down. My life was unrecognizable. I had been dancing four to five days a week and hung out frequently with friends. I also had a list of all the museums in DC I would visit before I moved to New Haven that fall. At the beginning of the pandemic, I found myself wondering how something like this could happen. I was studying the spread and distribution of diseases and health. I had never imagined living through a pandemic. It was our job to prevent them. That is what Public Health does. We had too many organizations in place for something like this to happen. I was confused.

I had not had cable television since my freshman year in college because I do not watch much TV. I also had my brother's Netflix account available if I ever found myself craving it. I usually watched nature documentaries or cartoons. It is difficult for me to take in all the information cable TV spews out. I did not have any knowledge of the spread of the virus until we received an email from the president of the university, advising us to go home for spring break and not return if possible. I instantly became concerned. Now it was on our campus. Three students tested positive. The administration had to take the necessary steps.

I stayed in DC during spring break. Going home was too expensive, and I did not technically live in student housing, so quarantining was easier for me. I constantly called my mom and cried, lamenting the loss of a life I had thought would never change. I was finally happy, loved where I was and who I was around, and now overnight my life was flipped upside down.

"Mom, everything was going perfectly. I don't understand." I sobbed, and she let me know that God had a plan for everything. She encouraged me to see that this was His way of slowing me down. I was in the best place in my life, but time was flying. Months felt like weeks. Weeks felt like days. The city life was good, but it moved very quickly. It took a few months, and I was eventually able to go home and spend time with my family. It was the first time since starting college in 2013 that I was able to spend that much quality time with my family, and I had not realized how much I missed it.

It was a tough year for me, 2020. But it opened my eyes to so much I would not have seen otherwise. I was sad that I would no longer be able to dance and hang out with my friends and even sadder that the experience as an incoming PhD student at Yale was taken from me. But grateful for so much. Unfortunately, many people were hurting. I lost two family members and had friends dealing with loss as well. It wasn't until I moved to New Haven that I finally felt like things were getting slightly back to normal.

I did not have to move to New Haven because classes were online. But I had spent enough time with my family to know I needed my own space to work. I took six classes over the summer, to finish my MPH in Epidemiology at GW by July 31 and start classes at Yale on August 1.

The possibility of making this dream a reality became very slim back in May when I tested positive for COVID. That moment was the most devastating. I had sensed something was wrong. I'd just returned to DC to start packing my apartment and finish my final papers at GW. My sister and her husband threw a party with only a few people, but I was not being safe. No one at the party seemed to have symptoms. But after the event ended, multiple people from the party ended up testing positive for COVID, even me.

When I got back to DC, I started to feel very weak. First, I had an upset stomach, which I found strange because I could not eat anything but was constantly going to the restroom. Next, I gradually lost my sense of taste and smell. I found that strange because I did not have a congested nose.

Everything came crashing down when I was in the middle of class (all classes were online at this point) and could not stay awake. I had gotten ten to twelve hours' sleep but still felt tired immediately after waking up. I had to stand up while working, just so I didn't doze off. I asked the professor to be dismissed early to go get tested. She agreed.

In the hot DC summer sun, praying that they didn't run out of testing kits because I was uninsured, I stood in line for two hours. I was usually covered under my mom's health insurance, but earlier that year she had stopped working, and we all lost coverage. When the doctor called me two days later, I was scared—but not surprised—to learn I tested positive for COVID. It felt like there was a sack of sand on my chest, and I could not stay awake to save my life. I alerted my siblings and close friends, and they all called me that minute. We were on a seven-way call, and they made jokes. But I knew their concern.

My family has a strong sense of humor; they always make light of a tough situation—a coping mechanism from our tough childhood. A friend brought me soup because it was the only thing I could eat at the time. She dropped it by my door, and I made sure she was gone before I opened the door. I realized then how important my relationships were.

Until I got better and tested negative, Eric called me every day outside of his busy work schedule to check on me. Although we had broken up, wc still remained close friends while I was living in DC and he in North Carolina. I hated the situation but am glad I got one more chance to see how truly blessed I am. I chose not to tell my mom until I got over it so I wouldn't worry her. I have tested negative every time since, but I am extra cautious now because that was a terrible experience. It was rough.

Though it was a mild case, being up there without family made it harder. My friends really helped me, and as I got over the worst part of the illness, I started to have more feelings of gratitude for my life, realizing how close I was to losing it.

When I finally moved to New Haven a few months later, I felt like I had made it to the promised land. It made me realize another basic principle: "I sought the LORD, and he answered me; he delivered me from all my fears" (Psalm 34:4). I had nothing to be afraid of. I always felt as if I was meant to be here at Yale, even more so after the first week of classes. I kept thinking the classes would be awfully hard—that I would struggle to keep up—but that didn't happen. What did happen, however, was something greater.

I still wanted to get the full experience of being a Yale PhD student, although classes were online. A part of me moved here because I thought if I could be on campus, then maybe the reality of my dreams being fulfilled would hit me. I moved to New Haven a little over a month before classes started. I packed up my entire apartment in DC alone. After eight long hours, I had finally managed to move my sofa, bed, and everything else into the back of the U-Haul truck. My feet were swollen for a week, and from moving the heavier items I had scratches and bruises all over my legs and arms. It was not easy, but I found out then that humans are capable of doing a lot more than what we may think. I drove the U-Haul to New Haven and hired the movers my landlord recommended when I got here because they only charged students $15 to move their stuff out of the U-Haul into the apartment. I paid them $100 each because that was easily an $800 job. I know, as I received a quote from a moving company the day before.

My one-bedroom apartment in New Haven was perfect! It was in a skyrise downtown and faced the east. I appreciated that feature because it made me wake up a lot earlier, with a great view of Yale's campus and the city. The sunrises were breathtaking, and I caught them more often than at any earlier moment in my life. My mom told me that my apartment facing the east was God's way of telling me I was meant to be there, and I felt every bit of that. My mindset completely changed once at Yale.

I walked around campus the first few days—filled with an overwhelming sense of gratitude, and some lingering feelings of guilt. However, there was a new feeling present. I remember packing up my pink-and-white beach blanket. Also, I took my journal, sunglasses, and a water bottle—to sit out on the green space in front of the Sterling Memorial Library, like I had seen in videos of Yale's campus or "A Day in the Life: Yale Student." With everything packed in my cloth bag, I took the elevator from the top floor to the lobby. I was distracted with my phone as the doorman was waving good-bye because I had no idea where the library was. I knew my GPS was my best option. As I tried my best not to look completely lost while walking around campus, I could not help but feel so happy. My mask covered the smile I had on my face that I'm sure stretched from ear to ear. "I am a Yale student. I am a Yale student," I said to myself over and over again as I walked around campus, trying to convince myself I was in the right place. The monolithic, pseudo-Gothic style buildings were beautiful—even more breathtaking than in the videos on YouTube.

When I finally made it to the green space in front of the library, I spread out my blanket and took a deep breath in as I sat there, marveling at the beauty of the campus around me. There were not many students on campus, but I enjoyed that vacant feeling. It gave me an even greater chance to take it all in.

At certain points, I found myself wondering if people would actually believe I was a student there. "What if someone walks up to me and tells me to leave? Do I even look smart enough to be a Yale student? Do I fit in?" I thought to myself.

It's funny how the mind will try to discourage you if you let it. That is why it is important to control the mind and your emotions. Mindfulness allows you to tap into that Silent Self and become more aware of who you are so that when questions like "Am I enough?" arise, you will automatically know that you are. You do not have to force out those negative thoughts. Using resistance only reinforces those feelings of inferiority. You must cancel and replace them with positive ones and positive emotions.

Emotions are never good or bad. Shakespeare once wrote: "there is nothing either good or bad but thinking makes it so." This is true. There are no good or bad emotions, for they are all valid; however, they can be positive or negative. The description refers to the type of energy they release. Positive emotions give you more energy, whereas negative emotions make you feel drained or unworthy. It is important to make that distinction. I allow negative emotions to run their course, and then I use the techniques I developed in therapy and through personal development books and videos to help me release them.

Over the span of the semester, I eventually convinced myself I was meant to be there because I started to develop a greater sense of self. I took classes like Black Theology, Theology and Medicine, Advanced Topics in Social and Behavioral Sciences, and Research Ethics. I had more room to take interesting electives because I was able to transfer courses from my MPH program. When my advisor told me that I could graduate early, I paused. I have been a student for so long, and so much of my identity has been wrapped up in being a lifelong learner that the thought of this educational journey coming to end frightened me initially.

The virtual classroom was tricky, and during election week 2020, several of my professors canceled class because emotional stress was so high. Once the semester ended, I realized something very valuable: this whole time, I was the one reason for my limiting beliefs. It hit me like a ton of bricks. I was keeping up in classes, even in my Theology and Medicine course, where we had to read a book almost every week, and no one ever questioned if I was good enough.

I remember being put into groups in that class, and on this one day, I was paired with Paul. When we got into our Zoom breakout rooms, he looked at me and said with a smile, "I have been waiting to get into a group with you. You're so intelligent, and I love the perspective you take on certain topics." A similar situation came up a few weeks later when I was paired with Mary. She was very vocal in class and energetic. So, I knew I could learn a lot from her. However, when in breakout rooms she said, "Oh wow! I am so happy I got to pair with you. You're insanely smart. and I know you will offer an interesting perspective on the question Professor Duke posed. What do you think? I would love to find out what you got from this week's readings!"

I was shocked because I never really considered myself a genius. I practice self-reflection daily, and my introverted personality makes it easier to do this, but I would often think, "How did I get here? What steps allowed me to make it from public housing to an Ivy League school like Yale?" I come to a similar conclusion each time. Aside from the Grace of God, which covers everyone who believes and even those that do not, it was passion and dedication that helped me. Writing this book was the first time in my life where I actually paused and thought about the entire journey at once. I have always been so focused on the future that I never paid much attention to past events or even present ones. I had a friend in DC ask me one day after class, "Have you stopped to look around at where you are?" Up until that point, I hadn't.

Intelligent people are everywhere. Everyone knows something that you do not, and in graduate school, I always felt like so many people were smarter than I. I had below-average test scores, after all. It took me a while to realize what being smart and intelligent actually was. My high-school mentor and JROTC instructor, First Sergeant Hill, called me one day, and we spoke for hours about this next chapter in my journey:

"I am so proud of you for reaching your goals and getting into Yale. You stepped up to the plate and played full out. Remember what I used to always tell y'all in class? Not everyone is willing to step up, but you don't step down if they are not willing to meet you where you are."

"Yeah, but there are so many other people that are smarter than me and could have gotten into an Ivy League too if they wanted to. They could accomplish whatever goals they held in their mind. I was not the smartest person in high school, by any means."

He stopped me and asked, "What is smart? If you have all the intelligence but choose to stay in a limiting situation and not push past the barriers, is that smart? Being smart means that you are willing to do whatever it takes, using the information you have, to have a better life and contribute. That is true intelligence."

I remember, before applying to Yale, attending the 2019 American Public Health Association (APHA) Meeting and Expo conference, "the largest and most influential yearly gathering of public health professionals," where I presented my research on a poster presentation called *Improving the Well-Being of African Americans through Religious Research*. I discussed the analysis I had conducted during my first master's degree, where I assessed data from a nationally representative sample from the Midlife Development in the U.S. (MIDUS) study.

I wanted to find out if religion and spirituality were protective against the negative health outcomes often common among low-income minorities. What I found was astonishing and was consistent with research in a similar area. Using a sample of African Americans from Milwaukee, I found that in low-income households, individuals who had higher religious/spiritual practices reported better physical health than those from similar-income households who had low levels of religiosity/spirituality. For my dissertation, I plan to further explore this association.

I knew Professor Yusuf Ransome of Yale (now my current advisor), previously mentioned in the introduction, also conducted religious/spiritual-based research. He was scheduled to be at that conference, and I took it as a perfect opportunity to meet him and find out more about his current research. His religious/spiritual studies were not posted on his website, but I found out from another professor at Yale that he had interests in that subject. I always encourage students to reach out to prospective graduate programs because sometimes you will find out more about research opportunities than you can find out online.

Dr. Ransome agreed to meet with me at the APHA conference. We would meet outside one of the conference rooms at 2:00 p.m. I was there at 1:30. I waited outside our designated spot and eventually sat down against the wall, there being no chairs available. APHA is a huge conference, and I experienced mental and physical fatigue. I sat there, thinking about all the things I would ask him and maybe imagining what his demeanor would be like because I had terrible experiences with professors who went to Ivy Leagues in the past.

Before too long, a well-dressed, tall, medium-framed man walked out of the conference room. I got to my feet with a big smile, realizing it was him. We had found a vacant conference room to meet in and spoke there before attending a session together. Almost two hours passed before the conclusion of our initial meeting. Dr. Ransome was so humble and genuine, and I could not believe we had so much in common, down to the videos we watched on YouTube of Dr. Myles Munroe and Les Brown. He was from the Caribbean, but our backgrounds were so similar. By the end of our talk, he looked at me and said the words I reported previously: "I could use your passion and drive in my lab."

I paused in disbelief at what he stated. "I just want to make sure I understand," I said, "You want me to come to Yale to work with you or stay at my current school and collaborate that way?"

He chuckled and said, "Yes, I want you to come to Yale. Go ahead and finish your application and submit it to the program, and I will keep an eye out for it." My eyes instantly welled with tears. I could feel the excitement boiling up in my stomach, like the feeling you get right before the roller coaster drops. At that moment, I knew that my passion and drive brought me this far, intellect was only a byproduct.

As mentioned earlier, nothing is as impossible as it may seem, but it all starts with you and how you think about a situation. Maybe your dream looks totally different than mine. It should! I assure you that your Truth will not directly map onto mine, and that is okay. Greatness is not what you have but what you give. Dr. Martin Luther King put it so powerfully when he said: "You're going to be deciding as the days and the years unfold what you will do in life, what your life's work will be. Once you discover what it will be, set out to do it and to do it well. Be a bush if you can't be a tree. If you can't be a highway, just be a trail. If you can't be the sun, be a star, for it isn't by size that you win or you fail, be the best of whatever you are."

What does your promised land look like? Hold that image in your mind and work toward it daily. Even on days when you do not feel like it. Those are the days that you must push even more. There is never a perfect time to start working on your dreams. Do not allow your mind to trick you into thinking that when it is your time to move toward your goal, everything will be perfect. The timing is never perfect. You must take action right here, right now and do the best you can with what you are given.

Rumi said, "What you seek is also seeking you," so when you start in the direction of your dreams you will be met with greater opportunities to succeed at them. We have consistently chosen fear disguised as practicality. Why not take a chance on faith right now? Both faith and fear require you to believe in something you cannot see. You have a choice as to which one you will follow. In his USC commencement speech, Jimmy Lovine stated, "When you learn to harness the power of your fears, it can take you places beyond your wildest dreams."[10] I have more peace in life knowing that I am using my gift to serve others as well as myself. Knowing that as I seek to serve, I am simultaneously being sought to be served by the abundance of this universe. I pray that my life reflects the joy I have found in seeking Truth and walking in it. I want to serve as a messenger of hope.

Action Steps and Ideas Worth Noting:

1. You can truly have anything you want if the desire is strong enough to cause you to take action.

2. You are good enough to be in the places you aspire to be in. Never question your self-worth because of your background, race, gender, etc. YOU ARE ENOUGH. End of story. You were created to be enough.

3. You do not have to accomplish big things to be successful. Whatever it is that you do, do it well and do it with love.

4. The perfect time to start working on your dreams is never coming. Do it now, and if you're scared, then do it with the fear. It will soon disappear when you realize that you are doing the things you once feared.

5. Both faith and fear require a belief in something we cannot see.

Chapter 8

Push Past the Barriers

There is no satisfaction that can compare with looking back across the years and finding you've grown in
self-control, judgment, generosity, and unselfishness.

—*Ella Wheeler Wilcox*

When Roger Bannister broke through the 4-minute mile barrier at 3 minutes 59.4 seconds on May 6, 1954, in Oxford,
England, it taught us more about the limits of conventional thinking
than anything else had previously. For decades, runners tried to break
the 4-minute mark, but over and over again without success. However,
after it had been done by Roger, it took only forty-six days for an Aus-
tralian runner, John Landy, to best it, at 3 minutes 58 seconds. John
not only broke the 4-minute barrier, but he ran it over half a second
faster than Roger. So, what changed? I will tell you.

More than a physical barrier, it was a psychological barrier that
broke. Sometimes all you need to see is one person do it so that you
can realize it's possible. That is, all we truly need to believe is that *it's
possible*. When I had just gotten to George Washington University in
2019, I had my first Black female professor. Not only was she African
American, but also, she had graduated from Yale and had been inter-
viewed on several news programs about her ideas on health policy and
management. The icing on the cake was that she had natural hair, just
like me. The second I walked into her classroom, something shifted. A
barrier was broken because I had seen it was possible. If she did it, then
I had a chance, too.

I believe there are two forms of success. First, objective success, which is what we commonly see on television and read about in magazines. Objective success refers to materialistic things that we acquire on our journey that others see, after we fulfill our dream, as an indication of possibility realized. It is the success that others place on you by observing what you gained in your pursuit of a better life. On the other hand, we have subjective success. This can only be measured by the individual. I would argue that out of the two, it is the most important.

There is a universal truth in the Holy Bible that states: "For what does it profit a man to gain the whole world, and forfeit his soul?" (Mark 8:36). I take that to mean, what is the value of having everything you ever desired if you do not know who you are?

Having self-awareness is a testament to that subjective success. You can have both, but they can exist separately as well. As Team Dan Lok remarks on his website, quoting Earl Nightingale: "Success is really nothing more than the progressive realization of a worthy ideal. This means that any person who knows what they are doing and where they are going is a success. Any person with a goal towards which they are working is a successful person."[11]

Barriers and obstacles will be ever-present. It is inevitable. However, you will overcome these obstacles sooner, once you decide not to take "no" for an answer and realize that the tree is already inside of you. It has always been there. Sometimes you just need the right environment to cultivate it so that you can bear good fruit.

Popular author and motivational speaker Jim Rohn (*The World Is Yours*) titled a YouTube video, "The Major Key to Your Better Future is You."[12] If you want an above-average life, develop yourself to become above average. I had never read a book a week in my entire life, but I knew if I wanted to do well as a first-year student at Yale, I would have to change that habit. This made me stop watching television and limit my time on social media to the weekends.

I had been using it to create and draw attention to my platforms, promoting my work and networking. Creating posts takes hours. The average time spent networking daily by internet users is two hours and twenty-two minutes.[13] Afterward, I became very interested in reading, and now it is my favorite leisure activity. Books have revealed a world of possibilities far beyond what I thought existed. I never understood why my dad enjoyed reading so much up until this point in my life.

Barriers are illusions that are only put there to sharpen your mental agility. If you are facing some of the same trials over and over again, take time to think about what that situation is trying to teach you. Did you grow from it the first time? If so, how?

Write down your lessons. I have kept a journal since the eighth grade and having one has saved me by allowing me to express everything I was feeling at the time. That in turn helped me clarify a mental picture of who I was becoming. Nothing compares to the feeling you get when you go back and read an entry from three years ago or sometimes even a month ago. It is easier to assess your progress when you can see it written down. Goals become clear when you download them out of your head and onto paper. When goal-setting, those who write down their goals are even more likely to have success in getting to where they want to go. There is a brain-to-hand connection that occurs in the process.

By offering clarity and pointing students to the right resources that will help them succeed, I coach students on how to navigate through higher education. I have been working as a certified Academic Success Coach for a few years now, and I find a common issue among my students. A lot of them do not know what they want out of their educational experience. How could they, when most of them are studying topics they think will make them a lot of money or that their family feels is most appropriate for them? I have only met a few students who were actually passionate about what they were learning, and they were rarely the students that I coached.

Security does not exist. People have lost secure jobs, relationships, and other things. Opportunity is where certainty lives. If you seek opportunity and not security, you will discover the beauty of life. When Jim Carrey was younger, he watched his dad forego his passion for comedy, taking a safe job as a consultant. When Jim was a teenager, his father was fired from that safe job; their family lost everything. He said, "I learned a lot of valuable lessons from my father. One of which being that you can fail at what you don't want, so you might as well take a chance at what you do want."[14]

We see successful people living out their dreams, and we try to place a divider between them and us. The truth is, there is no difference between you and the people you see on television—and those you do not see—who obtained success. There is no such thing as an extraordinary person who did not make sacrifices and push past the illusion of limitation. Limitations exist only in your mind. Expand your thinking, and this will allow you to expand the possibilities for your life. You expand your thinking through educating yourself.

Each time I made it to the other side of any barrier, I always whispered to myself, "Okay, you made it. You can rest now." I would rest initially, but I was soon met by another barrier or possible goal. There is always a worthy goal worth pursuing. Because I have attached myself to the mission of serving others by using the gift of education, I constantly discover possibilities available to achieve that mission. You must always search for information and self-knowledge because the human spirit's will is to expand. It is a limitless force within the limits of our physical body. Once your physical body makes it even further and your horizon begins to expand, the human spirit, if aligned with your Divine Purpose, will coach you in the direction of possibilities.

I have tried several times to ignore the call because I only wanted to go to school and learn. I never imagined myself making an impact through informational videos, interviews, or even this book! I later learned that it is important for me to share the knowledge I was gaining. What is the point of gathering all this information and going through everything that could have stopped me from reaching my goals if I cannot share that gift with others? "Each of you should use whatever gift you have received to serve others, as faithful stewards of God's grace in its various forms" (1 Peter 4:10). The effect you have on others, I believe, is the most valuable currency there is. Everything else you gain in life, materialistically, will rot and fall apart.

Clarity is power. Discovering who I was and what gifts I was willing to offer to improve this world was the greatest form of clarity God revealed to me. It took time and dedication, and I am discovering more and more about myself every day. We are not meant to stop growing. Every day is a chance to improve if you are intentional about your personal growth. While you are on this journey of self-discovery, please understand that not everyone will be happy to see you grow. Some people become uncomfortable with your growth because now they have to learn how to manipulate and communicate with you all over again. Personal development impacts everyone and everything around you. Keep expanding your consciousness because this challenges others to do the same. Nothing you do will affect just you. Additionally, nothing you do can grow unless you do.

At the end of 2020, I decided to attend a three-day virtual summit designed to prepare the attendees for the year to come. Over those three days, I had the opportunity to listen to motivational speakers and connect with other coaches and entrepreneurs, including Mike Sherbakov, a military veteran, now an expert in areas like social entrepreneurship, digital marketing, community building, and leadership development. Out of all the speakers, Mike said something that stuck with me for a very long time. He said that before he decided to pursue his goal of starting his business, he had struggled with self-doubt.

He had the idea for a long time but could not push past the fear of failure. One day, looking at himself in the mirror, he said, "I wish I had the courage to live a life that is true to myself, and not the life others expect for me." [15]

I thought, *"Courage? That is what it takes to live your dreams."* Not many people fully understand that aspect of being successful, that it takes courage.

Philosopher/writer Ralph Waldo Emerson once stated that you become what you think about all day long.[16] Great thinkers, scientists, theologians, and philosophers disagree on many topics, but one thing they all agree on is that you truly do become what you think. Everything begins and ends in your mind. You see the world through your mind's eye—"the mental faculty of conceiving imaginary or recollected scenes"[17]—which means your perception of life determines your reality.

In short, the quality of your life depends on the quality of your thoughts.

So, I encourage you to use your creativity and imagination to create a world full of abundance and opportunity. You only have to ACT AS IF.

Now, the "act" is very important because action makes the difference between those who achieve and those who do not. As I mentioned earlier, information alone cannot cause transformation. If it could, then many people would be happy, in tiptop shape, and rich who are not.

It takes action—the application of the information—to move from where you currently are to where you want to be in life. Fear will ALWAYS be present, but it is up to you to push past it. Are you in control of your fear, or is your fear in control of you? As the motivational writer David Joseph Schwartz so elegantly puts it, "Do what you fear, and fear disappears."[18]

Taking the steps towards living out my dreams as a graduate student, army officer, entrepreneur—and now author—were all hugely fearful for me. However, if I did not try, then I knew I would not be happy. I used to live in fear of what others would think of me. I was used to limiting myself, even though I had convinced myself for a long time that I was not.

My journey of self-discovery is not over. In fact, I feel it is just starting. This next adventure I will start with a strong sense of self because now I know where I come from, and I have a better idea of where I am going. My background is one of resiliency, and my future is one of hope.

In this next chapter of my life, I will take with me the skills I have developed, and continue to develop, up until this point. I have attached myself to the mission of service to others in its various forms. Although I do have a plan for my life, as I always had, I trust that the Lord will direct my path. In the words of Tracy Kidder, "Don't worry about being worried. You're heading out on an adventure and you can always change your mind along the way and try something else." The most fulfilling part of my journey is knowing that I am supported by the abundance of this universe, and now that I know who I am, nothing seems impossible.

I have made it beyond where I wanted to be, and now my focus is on serving others to help them get to where they want to be. People tried to get me to believe that my dreams were not possible, and I was rejected by over half a dozen schools before coming to Yale. It was hard, but I did it hard! I had to take the road less traveled, and I lost people I never thought I would on my journey of self-discovery. I could not do what was normal, and I never wanted to. I am happy with where and who I am now because I choose to live a life that will outlive me, and this is only the beginning of my becoming.

You must become *crystal clear* on what it is you want out of life. You gain that clarity by investing in your personal development and by facing your biggest fears. The beautiful thing about this is that you do not have to do it on your own. So, what are you waiting for? Your Higher Self has been waiting on you!

Action Steps and Ideas Worth Noting:

1. Barriers are illusions. They do not exist in real life, because people constantly break barriers and show others that breaking them is possible.

2. Consider the forms of success proposed in this chapter: objective and subjective success. Which one is more important to you? Why?

3. Start keeping a journal. Practice writing in it as often as possible. I would suggest starting weekly and move to daily writing, once you are used to putting your thoughts on paper. Going back to read your past thoughts will provide insight into your goals and help you gain greater clarity on who you are. You truly are a sum total of your thoughts.

4. Those who write down their goals when goal setting are even more likely to have success getting to where they want to go. There is a brain-to-hand connection that occurs in the process.

5. Use whatever gifts you have to serve others. You become clear about your gifts through self-awareness.

6. "I wish I had the courage to live a life that is true to myself, and not the life others expect for me." Are you living a life that is true to yourself? You are the only one who knows the answer to that question. There is no substitute for self-awareness.

Epilogue

I have written this book out of my deepest desire to serve. People often ask me, "How did you do it?" I hope that question is now answered, and you were able to see that getting over $670,000 in scholarship awards took dedication and persistence. Finishing two master's degrees in three years took dedication and persistence. Making it into my dream school at Yale University took dedication and persistence. Developing the courage to live out my dreams took dedication and persistence. I do not know any other way.

Investing in my personal development and educating myself with practical skill sets, like financial literacy and emotional intelligence, complemented the traditional classroom education I was receiving. My prayer is that you are able to see the many parts of chasing a dream.

I stated earlier that success is the "progressive realization of a worthy ideal." Additionally, you must delete the phrase "secret of success" and replace it with "*system of success.*" You tap into that system by developing the right mindset. Model the system of success of those who have gone before you, adjust that system to fit your individual needs.

Remember, never allow someone to push their insecurities onto you. You are enough because you were created to be enough. Seek the Truth for yourself by asking questions. When you find the answers, ask more questions. *This will allow you to know yourself so well that you will not be shaken when someone, looking through a lens of limitation, does not see the vision for your life.* Allow faith to carry you to victory! When you are walking in your vision, others will eventually see it. I believe in you, but most importantly, I need you to believe in you. That is when miracles happen and dreams are fulfilled. I wish you well on your journey to self-discovery, and God bless.

Endnotes

1   M. J. Murphy, L. C. Mermelstein, K.M. Edwards, & C. A. Gidycz (2012), "The benefits of dispositional mindfulness in physical health: A longitudinal study of female college students, *Journal of American College Health*, 60(5), 341–348; J. Schneider, P. Malinowski, P. M. Watson, & P. Lattimore (2019), "The role of mindfulness in physical activity: A systematic review," *Obesity Reviews*, 20(3), 448–463; E. Seppälä (2017), "How meditation benefits CEOs," *Harvard Business Review*, https://hbr. org/2015/12/how-meditation-benefits-ceos.

2   As quoted on Goodreads. Napoleon Hill, *Think and Grow Rich! The Original Version, Restored and Revised*™.

3   Les Brown said this during one of his live sessions for his Power Voice Program this past December 2020. Les is my coach right now, so I reference him a lot. I met with his program weekly. It is also something he said in his famous Georgia Dome speech. Available on YouTube.

4   Les Brown.

5   "If you are willing to do only what's easy, life will be hard. But if you are willing to do what's hard, life will be easy" is first attributed to T. Harv Eker.

6   Gina Milicia, website, A comfort zone is a beautiful place, but nothing ever grows there - Gina Milicia.

7   *The Letters of Vincent Van Gogh*.

8   This was a Facebook comment on his page.

9   In January 1988 "Ms." magazine credited the remark to Roosevelt.

10 In his USC commencement speech, https://www.hollywoodreporter.com/ear-shot/read-jimmy-iovines-usc-commencement-525328,https://www.hollywoodre-porter.com/earshot/read-jimmy-iovines-usc-commencement-525328.

11 Team Dan Lok, What's Your Definition of Success? (danlok.com).

12 (315) Jim Rohn: The Major Key To Your Better Future Is You - YouTube.

13 Denis Metev, "How Much Time Do People Spend on Social Media?" https://review42.com/resources/how-much-time-do-people-spend-on-social-media/#:~:-text=Internet%20users%20spend%20an%20average,to%20be%20on%20social%20media.

14 Jim Carrey Commencement Address in 2014 at Maharishi University of Management, https://www.youtube.com/watch?v=V80-gPkpH6M.

15 Google has it as a quote from the book: *The Top Five Regrets of the Dying* by Bronnie Ware.

16 "Inspiration Feed," 30 Best Ralph Waldo Emerson Quotes To End Your Day On a Good Note - Inspirationfeed.

17 Merriam-Webster.

18 "David J. Schwartz: World Renowned Authority on Motivation," David J. Schwartz Home Page - Biography and book listing (wwwhubs.com).

Acknowledgments

I am not sure how I could thank the many people who poured their energy and belief into me and helped me manifest my vision. To my mother, thank you. Your prayers and love helped me through so much, including the process of writing this book. When I was a struggling grad student, you helped me see that writing would be how I helped others and myself. To all my mentors and coaches who sacrificed time and resources to help me overcome all the obstacles placed in my path, thank you for always believing in me and seeing my light, even when I could not. It truly takes a village. To my father, thank you for your legacy. You are no longer physically with me, but I know your spirit never left. Your love for wisdom and understanding still lives on through me and all of your children.

About the Author

When Crystal Tammara Harrell realized that everything she needed to be successful was already inside of her, she started praying for the wisdom to use the gifts she already possessed. As a high-school senior, Crystal secured over $670,000 in scholarship awards, including the Bill and Melinda Gates Millennium Scholarship and the Army ROTC merit award.

She completed her Bachelor of Arts in Sociology in 2017, Master of Science in Human Development and Family Studies in 2018, and Master of Public Health in Epidemiology in 2020. She now attends Yale, where she is completing her PhD in Public Health, using her education as a gift to serve others through research and becoming a certified Academic Success Coach. Crystal also serves part-time as a First Lieutenant in the Army Medical Department, securing a leadership position in her current military unit.

Raised in rural Alabama on government assistance, Crystal is the seventh-born child of ten children. After her father died with cancer when she was eleven, her single mother did her best to provide for the family, which was not always easy. However, after years of persistence and dedication, Crystal's wildest dreams have come true as she beats the odds of being raised in poverty. Now her focus is on reaching back to help others out of the snares of adversity by sharing her story.

This book is Crystal's Truth and her offer to serve more people like herself. Those who feel inadequate because of their background. Those who suffer from impostor syndrome but know deep down their dreams can come true if they only have an opportunity.

Can You Help?

Thank You for Reading My Book!

I really appreciate all of your feedback, and I love hearing what you have to say.

I need your input to make the next version of this book and my future books better.

Please leave me an honest review on Amazon, letting me know what you thought of the book.

Thanks so much!

Crystal Harrell